A

OF

ST. MARK'S PARISH

CULPEPER COUNTY, VIRGINIA,

WITH NOTES OF

OLD CHURCHES AND OLD FAMILIES,

AND ILLUSTRATIONS OF THE

Manners and Customs of the Olden Time.

BY

REV. PHILIP SLAUGHTER, D. D.

Rector of Emmanuel Church, Culpeper Co., Va.

CLEARFIELD

Originally published
Baltimore, Maryland, 1877

Reprinted for
Clearfield Company, Inc. by
Genealogical Publishing Co., Inc.
Baltimore, Maryland
1994, 1998

International Standard Book Number: 0-8063-4793-7

Made in the United States of America

THE AUTHOR'S PREFACE.

The author believes that he was the first person who conceived the idea of writing a history of the old parishes in Virginia upon the basis of the old vestry-books and registers. Thirty years ago he published the History of Bristol Parish (Petersburg), of which he was then rector. In 1849 he published the History of St. George's Parish, in Spotsylvania. His labors were then suspended by ill-health, and he went abroad, never expecting to resume them. This personal evil resulted in the general good. Bishop Meade, the most competent of all men for this special task, was induced to take up the subject, and the result was the valuable work, "The Old Churches and Families of Virginia," in which the author's histories of St. George and Bristol Parishes, and some other materials which he had gathered, were incorporated. The author, in his old age, returns to his first love, and submits to the public a history of his native parish of St. Mark's. The reader will please bear in mind that this is not a general history of the civil and social institutions within the bounds of this parish, and yet he will find in it many incidental illustrations of these subjects. He must also be reminded that it does not purport to be a history of Christianity in its varied forms and polities within the lines of St. Mark's. That would open a large field, which the author has not time or strength now to traverse. He means, therefore, no disrespect to other Christian polities and peoples (among whom are numbered many valued friends and relatives) in omitting all reference to them. In this respect he has followed the example of the parish records, which are the bases of this history, and in which there is not one word about Christians of other names, from the first organization of St. Mark's Parish, in 1731, to the present moment. The vestry abstained in like manner from political allusion; for while keeping up its organization and records during the whole of the American Revolution, the only allusion to an event which so absorbed men's minds is the following entry:—" Capt. Richard Yancey is appointed a vestryman in place of Major John Green, in Continental service."

Church history in Virginia may 'be distributed into several eras, the observation of which will make it more intelligible. The first is the Era of the Church of England in the Colony and Dominion of Virginia. This covers the whole period from the first plantation of Jamestown to the American Revolution. During this period the Church was in bondage to the State, which never allowed it to organize. For political reasons it was not permitted to have a bishop; and there were no ordinations or confirmations during the whole colonial term. Candidates for orders had to make the then costly, protracted and perilous voyage across the sea. Some of them could not pay the expense, and others were lost at sea, while some died of the small-pox in London, which was very fatal before the use of vaccination. The Church was not only denied an executive head, but it had no legislature. It had no authority to pass a law, enact a canon, or inflict a penalty, not even for the discipline of its own ministers and members; and it never performed one of these functions.

The second era may be called the Transition Age, during which the ties that bound it to the State were one by one severed; and this lasted from 1776 to the first organization of the Protestant Episcopal Church of Virginia, in 1785, when it became free, although its organization was not perfected until the election of its first bishop (Madison).

The next era may be called the Era of Decline, when the Episcopal Church was staggering under the odium of having been an established church, which lasted until William Meade, William Wilmer, William Hawley, Oliver Norris, and such like, came upon the stage, and elected Richard Channing Moore, of New York, to be their leader. Then began the Era of Revival; after a torpid winter, an awakening spring followed by a fruitful summer. To this season we may apply the words of Shakspeare, but in a higher sense :—

"Now is the winter of our discontent
Made glorious summer by this son of *York;*
And all the clouds that lowered upon our house,
In the deep bosom of the ocean buried "—

While we recognize and rejoice in the good that has
been done by other Christian ministers outside of
our fold, we too may be permitted to rejoice that
our Virginian Episcopal Roll is "without a blemish ";
and that their hands have been upheld by a goodly
and growing company of preachers, who have re-
kindled the fires upon many an old altar where the
sparrow had found her an house, and the swallow a
nest for herself, even thine altars, O Lord God of
Hosts! my King and my God.

SUGGESTIONS TO OUR READERS.

In such an almost countless number of names and
dates as occur in this book, it must needs be that
errors of the pen or of the press will creep in. If
those who detect them will kindly communicate
them to the author, he will gladly correct them in a
new edition; the proposed first edition having been
ordered in anticipation of publication. If the reader
will bear in mind the following facts it will facilitate
his understanding of this history. In 1720 Spots-
sylvania County was taken from Essex, King and
Queen and King William, whose jurisdiction hitherto
extended to the great mountains. St. George's

Parish, coterminous with Spotsylvania, was formed by the same Act. In 1731 St. Mark's was taken from St. George. In 1734 Orange was formed from Spotsylvania. In 1740 St. Thomas was taken from St. Mark's. In 1748 Culpeper was formed from Orange. In 1752 Bromfield Parish was taken from St. Mark's. In 1792 Madison County was taken from Culpeper. In 1831 Rappahannock County was formed from Culpeper, and in 1838 the County of Greene was taken from the County of Orange.

ACKNOWLEDGMENTS.

Besides the acknowledgments made in the body of this work, the author is under obligations to Isaac Winston, Jr., for volunteering to transcribe his entire manuscript into a fair hand—a task almost as difficult as the interpretation of hieroglyphical characters by Oriental scholars. I am indebted for a like favor to Rev. Dr. Randolph, of Emmanuel Church, Baltimore, for volunteering to read the proof-sheets as they passed through the press; and to the Rev. Dr. Dalrymple, the Hon. Hugh Blair Grigsby, Mr. R. A. Brock, of the Virginia Historical Society, Dr. Andrew Grinnan, of Madison, Mr. George Mason Williams, of Culpeper, Col. Edward McDonald, of Louisville, to the gentlemen of the press, and to many correspondents too numerous to be named, for aid and sympathy in his work.

INDEX.

ST. MARK'S PARISH. PAGE

SIR ALEXANDER SPOTSWOOD, Lieutenant-Governor of Virginia:
His Ancestry, Birth, Marriage, Administration, Death, Burial,
Descendants, and Relation to St. Mark's Parish, . . . 1

ORGANIZATION OF ST. MARK'S PARISH, ... 6

FIRST MINISTER OF ST. MARK'S, ... 16

REV. JOHN THOMPSON, ... 18

CULPEPER COUNTY, ... 23

THE ORGANIZATION OF THE CHURCH IN VIRGINIA, . . . 45

REV. JOHN WOODVILLE, ... 49

REV. JOHN COLE, ... 62

THE SUCCESSORS OF THE REV. MR. COLE, ... 69

PRESENT STATUS OF THE CHURCHES IN ST. MARK'S, . . 71

ST. THOMAS PARISH, Orange County, ... 73

BROMFIELD PARISH, ... 79

HISTORICAL EXCURSIONS.

THE KNIGHTS OF THE GOLDEN HORSESHOE, ... 83

GERMANNA, ... 97

DIARY OF CAPTAIN PHILIP SLAUGHTER, beginning in 1775 and
continued to 1849, ... 106

LEWIS LITTLEPAGE, ... 109

THE TOBACCO PLANT, ... 114

GENEALOGIES.

THE BARBOUR FAMILY, ... 118

THE CARTER FAMILY, ... 121

THE CAVE FAMILY, ... 122

THE CLAYTONS, ... 125

THE COLEMANS, ... 128

THE CONWAY FAMILY, ... 129

The Fields, ... 130
The Fry Family, ... 132
The Garnett Family, ... 134
The Glassell Family, ... 136
The Green Family, ... 138 —
The Lightfoots, ... 142
The Madison Family, ... 144
The Pendleton Family, ... 148
The Slaughter Family, ... 157
The Spotswood Family, ... 165
The Rev. James Stevenson, ... 168
The Strother Family, ... 169
The Taylor Family, ... 172
Family of the Rev. John Thompson, ... 174
The Williams Family of Culpeper, ... 177
The Winston-Henry Genealogy, ... 183
Rev. John Woodville, ... 192
Lieut.-General Ambrose Powell Hill, ... 193
The Broadus Family, ... 194

MISCELLANEOUS ITEMS.

The Brown Family, ... 195
Medical Men in Culpeper before the Revolution, . . 195
The Lawyers, ... 196
Towns in Culpeper, ... 196
    Stevensburg; Clerksburg, not Clarksburg; Jefferson; Spring-
    field; Jamestown.
Brick Making in Virginia, ... 198
Vestrymen of St. Mark's, ... 198

St. Mark's Parish.

SIR ALEXANDER SPOTSWOOD,

LIEUTENANT-GOVERNOR OF VIRGINIA,

HIS ANCESTRY, BIRTH, MARRIAGE, ADMINISTRATION, DEATH, BURIAL, DESCENDANTS, AND RELATION TO ST. MARK'S PARISH.

A history of St. Mark's Parish, in which Governor Spotswood did not have a prominent place, would be like a portrait with the most prominent feature left out. Not only was he a sagacious statesman, a gallant cavalier, a brave and dashing soldier; but he was also a devout Church of England man, ready to enter the lists as her champion against all comers, not excepting the vestries, who were the advocates of the people's rights, and the miniature Parliaments in which the leading statesmen of the American Revolution were trained. He was the largest landed proprietor within the bounds of the parish; he founded the first town (Germanna), he developed the first mines, and erected the first iron furnace in America. He erected, chiefly at his own expense, the first parish church, and organized and equipped, at Germanna, "The Knights of the Golden Horseshoe," who first passed the Blue Ridge, and blazed the way to the Valley of Virginia, and whose whole

A

course was within the limits of the original parish of
St. Mark's.

Governor Spotswood was the great-grandson of
John Spotswood, Archbishop of St. Andrew's, and
author of the History of the Church of Scotland.
His grandfather was Robert Spotswood, Lord President of the College of Justice, and author of the
" Practicks of the Laws of Scotland," who was one
of the eight eminent lawyers executed by the Parliament of Scotland, which (according to Sir Walter
Scott) consisted wholly of Covenanters. While he
was at private prayer on the scaffold (says Sir Walter)
he was interrupted by the Presbyterian minister in
attendance, who asked if he did not desire his prayers
and those of the people. Sir Robert replied that he
earnestly desired the prayers of the people, but not
those of the preacher; for that, in his opinion, God
had expressed his displeasure against Scotland by
sending a lying spirit into the mouths of the prophets.
The father of Governor Spotswood was Dr. Robert
Spotswood, physician to the Governor of Tàngiers in
Africa, and his mother had been Mrs. Catherine
Elliott. Dr. Spotswood died at Tangiers in 1688,
leaving one son, the subject of this notice, who was
born in 1676. Governor Spotswood, " who had been
bred in the army," was aide to the Duke of Marlborough, and was badly wounded in the breast at the
battle of Blenheim.

His arrival in Virginia, says Campbell, was greeted
with joy, because he brought with him the right of
Habeas Corpus — a right guaranteed to every
Englishman by Magna Charta, but hitherto denied
to Virginians. Spotswood entered upon his duties as
Governor in 1710, and the two Houses of the General

Assembly, severally, returned thanks for their relief from long imprisonment, and appropriated more than two thousand pounds for completing the Governor's palace. Although he was, in accordance with the dominant doctrines of his day, a strenuous advocate of the Royal prerogative in Church and State, yet he was one of the most energetic, patriotic and far-seeing statesmen that ever ruled Virginia. He first suggested a chain of forts from the Lakes to the Mississippi (beyond the Alleghanies) to check the encroachments of the French; but many years elapsed before his suggestion and policy were adopted. It was he who conceived the idea of making tobacco notes a circulating medium. His military genius and experience enabled him to wield the militia with great effect against the hostile Indians; but he was no less zealous in the conception and execution of measures for their civilization and conversion to Christianity, as the Indian school at Christanna on the Meherin river, and the fund of £1000 for instructing their children at William and Mary College, attest. In 1739 he was made Deputy Postmaster-General for the Colonies; and it was he (says Campbell) who promoted Benjamin Franklin to be postmaster for the province of Pennsylvania.

Governor Spotswood died at Annapolis, on his way to command the army against Carthagena, and was buried at Temple Farm, one of his old country-seats near Yorktown, so named from a house in the garden erected by Governor Spotswood as a cemetery. Dr. Shield, who bought the farm in 1834, says, "the walls of the temple were then only several feet high: within them I found heaps of broken tombstones, and on putting the fragments together, I found the name of Governor Spotswood."

It was in the Temple Farm mansion that Lord Cornwallis met Washington and signed the articles of capitulation which secured American independence.

There is some verbal discrepancy between the authorities about the name of the lady whom Governor Spotswood married. Bishop Meade, upon the authority of a daughter of General Alexander Spotswood, says that her name was Jane Butler, sister of the Duke of Ormond. Charles Campbell, our painstaking historian, says her name was Butler Bryan (pronounced Brain), daughter of Richard Bryan, of Westminster, and her Christian name was after James Butler, Duke of Ormond, her godfather. On the other hand, several of her lineal descendants have informed the present writer that Mrs. Spotswood was the daughter of Richard *Brayne*, " whose letters to his daughter show him to have been a man of culture." The name of Butler *Brayne* has been perpetuated in this branch of the family to this day, which raises a strong presumption that it is the true orthography.

Since the above was written I have procured, through the medium of Judge Barton and Capt. George Minor of Fredericksburg, documentary proof which settles the vexed question, in the form of a letter written by Judge Edmond Pendleton for his client John Benger, the son of Dorothea (Col. Byrd's Miss Thecky) Brayne, sister of Lady Spotswood. The letter is dated Virginia, Sept. 8th, 1762, and is addressed to Capt. Wm. Fox, and is signed by John Benger and Edmond Pendleton, and in it is the following paragraph:—" Richard Brayne and his wife are dead, and Mrs. Brayne's issue was four daughters, Anne, Diana, Dorothy, and Butler. Dorothy intermarried with Elliot Benger, gentleman, and, with her husband, is since dead, and I am her son and heir. Butler intermarried with Major-General Alexander Spotswood, and afterwards married John Thompson (Clerk). She is dead, and Alexander Spotswood, infant, is her grandson and heir, and is now in England. Anne and Diana remained in England and never married."

Governor Spotswood had four children, John, Robert, Anne Catherine, and Dorothea. John married, in 1745, Mary, daughter of Capt. Dandridge, of the British army, and had two sons, General Alexander and Capt. John, both officers of the Revolution; and two daughters, Mary and Ann. John, son of John and grandson of the Governor, married Mary Rousee of Essex, and had many children. General Alexander Spotswood, grandson of the Governor, married Elizabeth, daughter of Augustine and niece of General Washington. Robert, second son of the Governor, was an officer under Washington in 1755, and was killed by the Indians. Anne Catherine (Kate) married Bernard Moore, of Chelsea in King William; and their daughter married Charles Carter of Shirley, and was the grandmother of our Chevalier Bayard (*sans peur et sans reproche*), General Robert Edward Lee, named after two of his uncles, Robert and Edward Carter.

Kate Spotswood, Mrs. B. Moore, was a great beauty. The late Mrs. Dunbar of Falmouth, a granddaughter of Lady Spotswood, had seen her, and was so impressed by the vision, that, with true womanly instinct, she remembered, after the lapse of many years, the details of her dress, which we reproduce for the benefit of our lady readers. It was a

fawn-colored satin, square in the neck, over a blue
satin petticoat, with satin shoes and buckles to
match, on very small and beautifully shaped feet.
A granddaughter of Kate, now living in a green old
age, says that when she was a little girl she saw
Kate sitting up in her bed at Chelsea, combing her
white and silken hair, with a servant holding up a
looking-glass before her.

There is a portrait of Governor Spotswood at
Chelsea, and there was another at Sedley Lodge in
Orange (now in the State Library at Richmond),
which the author of this historical tract had daguer-
reotyped. It represents him in full dress, scarlet
velvet — graceful and commanding in face and figure
— antique model of the cavalier — the old English
and the old Virginia gentleman, who are as much
alike as father and son. What a grand genealogical
tree!—with General Sir Alexander Spotswood its
root in Virginia, and Robert Edward Lee its bright,
consummate flower.

ORGANIZATION OF ST. MARK'S PARISH.

The Register of St. Mark's Parish, which lies
before me, is the oldest manuscript record in the
county of Culpeper. The parish is older than the
county by eighteen years, the former having been
established by Act of Assembly in 1730, and the latter
in 1748. It is curious to note the progress of population, and parishes and counties, from their original
seats on tidewater towards the mountains. The
people went before, the parishes followed after, and
the counties completed the organization, according

to the uniform policy of the British Government to keep the Church and State in union.

In 1634 the colony of Virginia was divided by the House of Burgesses into eight counties, or shires, as they were then called. In 1692 the old county of Rappahannock was extinguished, and its territory distributed into the counties of Richmond on the north, and Essex on the south, side of the Rappahannock River. The movement of the growing population was along the banks of the rivers, on account of the greater productiveness of the soil, and the facilities of transportation, in the absence of roads in the intervening wilderness. Thus early in the eighteenth century the settlement had passed the Falls of the Rappahannock and reached the Rapid Ann River, where a colony of Germans had seated themselves, and Lieutenant-Governor Spotswood had established a furnace and built a "castle," in which he occasionally resided.

Over the new settlement a new county and a new parish were erected in 1720. The preamble to the Act of Assembly declares that " the frontiers towards the high mountains being exposed to danger from the Indians and the French settlement towards the west, a new county is established, bordering upon Snow Creek up to the Mill, thence by a southwest course to the North Anna, thence up the said river as far as convenient, and thence by a line over the high mountains to the river Shenandoah, so as to include the North Pass through said mountains; thence down said river till it comes against the head of Rappahannock River, and down that river to the mouth of Snow Creek; which tract of land shall become a county by the name of Spotsylvania, and

the whole county shall be one parish, by the name of
St. George."

The Act also appropriated five hundred pounds for
a church, courthouse, pillory and stocks, where the
Governor shall appoint. Another clause appropri-
ates one thousand pounds for arms and ammunition,
to such " Christian tithables " as shall go to seat this
county. The county of Brunswick was established
by the same law. The inhabitants were made free
of levies for ten years. The same privilege is extended to Germans and other foreign Protestants,
" who may not understand English readily," if they
will entertain a minister of their own.

It will be observed that the movement of counties, parishes and people, by way of Spotsylvania
and Brunswick, was towards the northern and southern passes through the " high mountains," to trans-
cend which and see what lay beyond was the great
problem of the day.

The Rev. Hugh Jones, one of the Colonial clergy,
in his " Present State of Virginia," published about
1724, says:—" Beyond Governor Spotswood's furnace,
within view of the vast mountains, he has founded
a town called Germanna, from some Germans sent
over by Queen Ann, who are *now removed up further.*
Here he has servants and workmen of most handicraft trades, and he is building a church, courthouse,
and dwelling-house for himself, and with his servants and negroes he has cleared plantations about
it, proposing great encouragement for people to
come and settle in that uninhabited part of the
world, lately divided into a county."

Colonel Byrd, of Westover, on James River, an
accomplished gentleman, an adventurous traveller,

and inimitable humorist, visited Colonel Spotswood in 1732, and indites the following pleasant gossip on the occasion:

" The famous town of Germanna consists of Colonel Spotswood's enchanted castle on one side, and a baker's dozen of ruinous tenements on the other, where so many German families had dwelt some years ago, but are now removed ten miles higher, in the Fork of the Rappahannock, to land of their own. There had also been a chapel about a bow-shot from the Colonel's house, at the end of an avenue of cherry trees, but some pious people had lately burnt it down, with intent to get another built nearer their own homes. Here I arrived about three o'clock, and found only Mrs. Spotswood at home, who received her old acquaintance with many a gracious smile. I was carried into a room elegantly set off with pier glasses, the largest of which came soon after to an odd misfortune. Among other favorite animals which cheered this lady's solitude, a brace of tame deer ran familiarly about the house, and one of them came to stare at me as a stranger, but unluckily spying his own figure in the glass, he made a spring over the tea-table that stood under it, and shattered the glass to pieces, and falling back upon the tea-table, made a terrible fracas among the china. This exploit was so sudden, and accompanied with such noise, that it surprised me and perfectly frightened Mrs. Spotswood. But it was worth all the damage to show the moderation and good humor with which she bore the disaster. In the evening the noble Colonel came home from his mines, who saluted me very civilly; and Mrs. Spotswood's sister, Miss Thecky, who had been to meet him, *en cavalier*, was

so kind, too, as to bid me welcome. We talked over
a legend of old stories, supped about nine, and then
prattled with the ladies till it was time for a traveller
to retire. In the meantime I observed my old friend
to be very uxorious and exceedingly fond of his children. This was so opposite to the maxims he used
to preach up before he was married, that I could not
forbear rubbing up the memory of them. But he
gave a very good-natured turn to his change of sentiments, by alleging that whoever brings a poor gentle-
woman into so solitary a place, from all her friends
and acquaintances, would be ungrateful not to use
her and all that belongs to her with all possible ten-
derness. We all kept snug in our several apartments
till nine, except Miss Thecky, who was the house-
wife of the family. At that hour we met over a pot
of coffee, which was not quite strong enough to give
us the palsy. After breakfast, the Colonel and I left
the ladies to their domestic affairs, and took a turn
in the garden, which has nothing beautiful in it but
three terrace walks, that fall in slopes one below
another. I let him understand that, besides the
pleasure of paying him a visit, I came to be instructed
by so great a master in the mystery of making iron,
wherein he had led the way, and was the Tubal Cain
of Virginia. He corrected me a little there, saying
that he was not only the first in his country, but the
first in North America who had erected a regular
furnace; that they ran altogether on bloomeries in
New England and Pennsylvania till his example had
made them attempt greater works. He said that
the four furnaces now at work in Virginia circulated
a great sum of money for provisions, &c., in the adja-
cent counties. He told me that he had iron in sev-

eral parts of his tract of forty-five thousand acres of land, but that the mine he was at work upon was thirteen miles below Germanna. He raised the ore a mile from the furnace, and carted the iron, when made, fifteen miles to his plantation on Massaponax. He said that during his absence in England he had lost eighty slaves, his furnace was still the greater part of the time, and all his plantations ran to ruin. But he was rightly served for trusting his affairs to a mathematician (Mr. Graeme), whose thoughts were always ' among the stars.' The afternoon was devoted to the ladies, who conducted me through a shady lane to the river, and by the way made me drink some very fine water that issued from a marble fountain. Just behind it was a covered bench, where Miss Thecky often sat and bewailed her virginity. The river is about fifty yards wide, and so rapid that the ferry-boat is towed over by a chain, and therefore called the Rapidan." The Miss Thecky above-mentioned was evidently the sister of Mrs. Spotswood, who married Mr. Benger, a cousin of the Governor, and from whom some of the Minors and Frenchs of Spotsylvania are descended.

Governor Spotswood, after whom Spotsylvania was called, fixed the seat of justice at Germanna, which was named after the German settlement. The history of these Germans deserves further investigation. In 1717 they consisted of one hundred and thirty persons, in twenty-nine families, and anticipated a large accession to their number. In a petition to the Bishop of London and the English society for the propagation of the Gospel in foreign lands, they described themselves as very desirous of having the ministers of religion in their own tongue, " not

understanding English well." They invoke the aid
of the Bishops in England to procure for them and
ordain a young German minister, to assist and to
succeed their old pastor (Haeger), now seventy-five
years of age, and to send with him the Liturgy of
the Church of England translated into High Dutch,
which they are desirous to use in public worship.
They were exempted by the General Assembly from
the payment of parish levies. Dr. Hawks says that
the parish of St. George was created for them. This
is clearly a mistake. Colonel Byrd, in the passage
quoted above, says he saw in 1732 "the ruinous te n-
ements " which they had occupied at Germanna, and
adds that they had moved higher up to the Fork of
the Rappahannock, to land of their own, which must
mean the juncture of the Rapid Ann (often called
the Rappahannock in those times) and the Robinson, which is now in the county of Madison. I
believe I was the first to suggest that there was the
nucleus of the German population in Madison county
(see my History of St. George's Parish, 1747).
Bishop Meade adopts this suggestion, and refers to
an old gentleman in Culpeper who had told him that
in his boyhood he had often seen the Lutherans from
Madison, when they had no minister of their own,
come to Buck Run Church, in Culpeper, to receive
the Holy Communion. That old gentleman was the
venerable vestryman and watchful warden, the late
Samuel Slaughter, of Western View, in St. Mark's
Parish. I have initiated inquiries which I hope will
throw some light on this obscurity.

In May, 1730, the General Assembly, in view of
the inconveniences arising to the parishioners of St.
George's Parish by reason of the great length there-

of, divided it by a line running "from the mouth of the Rapid Ann to the mouth of the Wilderness Run; thence up the said run to the bridge, and thence southward to the Pamunkey River. All the territory above that line to be called and known as St. Mark's Parish." The same Act directs the freeholders and housekeepers of the new parish to meet at the new church in Germanna, on the first day of the following January, and elect twelve of the most able and discreet persons of the parish to be vestrymen of said parish. In pursuance of this Act, the freeholders and housekeepers did meet at Germanna on the 1st day of January, 1731, and elected Goodrich Lightfoot, Henry Field, Francis Kirtly (not Huntly, as in Bishop Meade's "Old Churches, &c."), William Peyton, James Barbour, Robert Slaughter, John Finlason, Francis Slaughter, Thomas Staunton, Benjamin Cave, Robert Green, and Samuel Ball. Robert Slaughter and Francis Slaughter were the first churchwardens, and William Peyton the first clerk.

These antique vestrymen were the fruitful germs of genealogical trees, which have scattered their prolific seeds from New York to Florida, and from Virginia to California. This is not a rhetorical flourish, but is literally true, and could be easily demonstrated, were "the play worth the candle." The progress of this narrative will furnish some suggestive illustrations of this truth.

1731. St. Mark's Parish now begins its independent career at Germanna, without a shepherd to seek after the flock scattered in the wilderness bounded by the Blue Mountains, which look so enchanting in the distance, when their summits are lighted by the

B

setting sun. There were three churches in the new
parish—one of them at Germanna, one in the Little
Fork, and one in the S. W. Mountain, in the neighborhood of Messrs. James Barbour and Benjamin
Cave, vestrymen. For the several years in which
they had no pastor the vestry employed occasionally
the Rev. Mr. De Butts and the Rev. Mr. Purit, two
adventurers who were seeking parishes, and paid
them three hundred pounds of tobacco per sermon.

In the absence of regular ministers, the churches
and chapels were served by Lay readers, or clerks, as
they were then called, whom the vestries seem
to have preferred to inefficient clergymen. The
vestry went vigorously to work, by ordering the
churches to be repaired and vestry-houses built; buy-
ing two hundred acres of land for a glebe, of Wm.
Ashley; contracting for a glebe-house, with all the
appurtenances of barns, stables, meat-houses, dairies,
&c. William Peyton was made Lay Reader at the
Little Fork; John McMuth had the double office of
clerk and sexton at Germanna; and William Philips
and David Cave, alternating clerks at the Southwest
Mountain Chapel. The churchwardens settled with
the old vestry of St. George's and bought parish
books. The parish lines were surveyed. Zachery
Lewis was chosen as their attorney. Robert Turner
was made collector of tithes. A. Chambers was
engaged to keep the church clean at Germanna;
John Carder to do the same office at the Fork, and
William Stevenson at the Mountain Chapel. Col.
Waller was employed to bring up a copy of the oaths
of allegiance to the British Crown, and of conformity
to the Church of England, and the test oath against
Popery — all of which the vestry had to take. Some

idea may be formed of the state of the country, from the fact that Augustine Smith, Jr., was paid 200 pounds of tobacco for *piloting* the minister to the Mountain Chapel, which was not far from Cave's Ford in Orange.

The vestry seem, too, to have been animated by a laudable spirit of church extension. Within two years (1732-1733) two churches and two chapels were projected. The first church was seated on what is now the road from Germanna to Stevensburg, "convenient to the springs above Major Finlason's path." This church, or one on the same site, was standing within the memory of men now living, and was used by the venerable Mr. Woodville. It is called, in the vestry book, the Lower or Great Fork Church. Mr. Spotswood, of Orange Grove, now in his 77th year, says he remembers when the Spotswoods, Gordons, Grymes, and Thorntons, near Germanna, used to attend this church. The other church was built "convenient to the Southwest Mountain road, on the first run below the chapel"; and John Lightfoot and John Rucker were ordered "to pitch on the place near to some good spring." This was the old church near Ruckersville, in the county of Green. Its age is left uncertain in Rev. Mr. Earnest's interesting article on St. Thomas's Parish in Bishop Meade's "Old Churches, &c." The old minister who first preached in this church, and whom Mr. Earnest could not identify, was either De Butts or Becket; both of whom were discharged by the vestry of St. Mark's. The first place of worship on the Southwest Mountain was a chapel, which James Barbour and Benjamin Cave undertook "to have kept clean." At the chapel, De Butts preached until 1732, at which date I find this

entry in the vestry book — "Ordered, that the Rev.
Mr. De Butts be paid 9000 pounds of tobacco for
thirty sermons." In December, 1733, a new chapel
was ordered, only twenty feet square, at Batley's, or
Bradley's, Quarter, "convenient to the best spring that
Benjamin Cave can find." Rev. Mr. De Butts, who
had been employed *by the sermon,* was now discharged,
and St. Mark's had its first elected minister in the
Rev. John Becket.

FIRST MINISTER OF ST. MARK'S.

May 11th, 1733, "ordered, that the Rev. J. Becket,
being recommended by the Governor and Commissary, be entertained as Minister of the Parish; and
that he receive the glebe and what is on it, and the
house when finished, and be paid as the law directs;
and that he preach at the Southwest Chapel every
other Sunday until further orders." At the next
vestry (1733) it was ordered that the churchwardens
offer the Hon. Col. Alexander Spotswood the choice
of a seat for himself and family in the church on the
Germanna road. In 1734, Major G. Lightfoot was
ordered to wait on Major John Taliaferro, to bring
up the surplice for Germanna Church. It was also
ordered that the church be painted and tarred, and
that S. Wright put four barrels of tar on the roof of
the glebe-house. In 1735 it was ordered that "a
chapel of ease" be erected and built between Shaw's
Mountain and the Devil's Run and the river; and that
Francis Slaughter, Robert Green, and Henry Field,
gentlemen, "pitch on the place most convenient to
the best spring that they can find, on one of the
branches of the run or river." Our fathers kept as

close to the rivers as if they had been amphibious, and kept as sharp a look-out for a good cool spring as Arabs do in the desert. They had ladles chained to the church-springs, and were careful to have good framed horse-blocks and bridle-hooks for those who went to church *en cavalier.*

Up to 1734-5, St. Mark's Parish was in Spotsylvania. At that date Spotsylvania was divided by the line between St. George's and St. Mark's Parishes. Spotsylvania was limited to St. George's Parish. All above that line, bounded southerly by old Hanover county, and to the north by the Lord Fairfax grant (the Rappahannock river), and westerly by the utmost limits of Virginia, was made the county of Orange. In 1738 John Catlett was added to the vestry in place of Goodrich Lightfoot, deceased. The Rev. J. Becket now came to grief for some scandalous conduct, and was discharged. In 1739 the church-wardens were instructed to agree with Mr. McDaniel to serve the parish, or with some other minister, *except Mr. Becket.* In 1738, Augusta and Frederick counties and parishes were separated from Orange and St. Mark's, by a line from the head-spring of Hedgeman's river to the head-spring of the Potomac, to take effect when there were people enough in the Valley for erecting courts of justice; and in the meantime, the people there were exempted from levies by Orange and St. Mark's. In 1740, St. Mark's was divided by a line from the Wilderness bridge up the mountain road, to the head of Russel Run; thence down the said run to the river Rapidan; thence up the Rapidan to the Robinson river; thence along the ridge, between the Robinson and Rapidan, to the top of the Blue Ridge. All north of said line to retain

the name of St. Mark's, and all south of said bounds
to be the new Parish of St. Thomas. This division
threw the Southwest Mountain Church and Chapel
into St. Thomas; and with them Messrs. James Barbour and Benjamin Cave, vestrymen. William Triplett and William Russell were elected to fill the
vacancies. We now reach the incumbency of the
first respectable minister in St. Mark's Parish.

REV. JOHN THOMPSON.

June 10th, 1740. Under this date is the following
entry in the Register:—"At a vestry in the vestry
house at the Fork: it is ordered, that the Rev. John
Thompson, being recommended by the Governor and
Commissary, we do entertain him as Minister of our
parish; and that he be paid as the law directs." Mr.
Thompson was a Master of Arts of the University of
Edinburgh. He had been ordained Deacon by the
Bishop of St. David's in the year 1734, at Westminster; and Priest in November of the same year,
in the Chapel Royal of St. James. It must have been
very pleasant to the gentlemen of the vestry and of
the parish, to have exchanged the former disreputable
incumbent for the accomplished gentleman. It seems
also to have been agreeable to one of the ladies of the
parish (if one may venture to say so, after all parties
have been so long dead); for the new minister was
not only a scholar and a literary gentleman, but he
was a very handsome man. The vestry testified
their pleasure by ordering a study to be added to the
glebe-house; and the widow of Governor Spotswood
presented a velvet cloth and cushion to the church
in 1741; and on the 9th of November, 1742, she vowed

to obey and to serve him in the holy estate of matrimony. Governor Spotswood's castle at Germanna, with its fair commander, did not surrender to the consummate address of the clerical besieger without a severe struggle, as the following letter will testify. I procured the original of this letter from Mrs. Murray Forbes of Falmouth, a lineal descendant of Mr. and Mrs. Thompson, and published it for the first time in my History of St. George's Parish, from whence it was copied by Bishop Meade in his "Old Churches and Families." Mrs. Spotswood's children and connections were so opposed to the match that she begged to be released from her engagement, and was answered thus:

MADAM,—

By diligently perusing your letter, I see that there is a material argument, which I ought to have answered, upon which your strongest objection to completing my happiness seems to depend, viz.: That you would incur ye censures of ye world for marrying a person of my station; by which I understand that you think it a diminution of your honour and ye dignity of your family to marry a person in the station of a clergyman. Now, if I can make it appear that the ministerial office is an employment in its nature ye most honorable, and in its effects ye most beneficial to mankind, I hope your objections will immediately vanish, y^t you will keep me no longer in suspense and misery, but consummate my happiness. I make no doubt, Madam, but y^t you will readily grant y^t no man can be employed in any work more honorable than what immediately relates to the King of kings and Lord of lords, and to ye salvation of souls immortal in their nature and redeemed by ye blood of the Son of God. The powers committed to their care cannot be exercised by ye greatest princes of earth, and it is ye same work in kind and ye same in ye design of it with y^t of the blessed angels, who are ministering spirits for those who shall be heirs of salvation. It is ye same business y^t ye Son of God discharged when he condescended to dwell among

men, which engages men in ye greatest acts of doing good in
turning sinners from the errors of their way, and by all wise
and prudent means in gaining souls unto God. And the faithful and diligent discharge of this holy function gives a title to
ye highest degree of glory in the next world; for they yᵗ be
wise shall shine as ye brightness of ye firmament, and they yᵗ
turn many to righteousness as the stars forever.

All nations, whether learned or ignorant, whether civil or
barbarous, have agreed to this, as a dictate of natural reason,
to express their reverence for the Deity and their affection for
religion, by bestowing extraordinary privileges of honour
upon such as administer in holy things, and by providing
liberally for their maintenance. And that ye honour due to
the holy function flows from ye law of nature appears from
hence, yᵗ in the earliest times the civil and sacred authority
were united in ye same person. Thus Melchisedech was King
and Priest of Salem, and among ye Egyptians ye priesthood
was joined with ye crown. The Greeks accounted the priesthood with equal dignity with kingship, which is taken notice
of by Aristotle in several places of his Politicks. Among the
Latins we have a testimony from Virgil yᵗ at ye same time
Æneas was both Priest and King. Nay, Moses, who was
Prince of Israel before Aaron was consecrated, officiated as
Priest in ye solemn sacrifice by which ye covenant with Israel
was confirmed. And ye primitive Christians always expressed
a mighty value and esteem for their clergy, as plainly appears
from ecclesiastical history. And even in our days, as bad as
ye world is, those of ye clergy who live up to ye dignity of
their profession are generally reverenced and esteemed by all
religious and well-disposed men. From all which it evidently
appears yᵗ in all ages and nations of ye world, whether Jews,
Heathens or Christians, great honour and dignity have always
been conferred upon the clergy. And therefore, dear Madam,
from hence you may infer how absurd and ridiculous those
gentlemen's notions are who would fain persuade you yᵗ marrying with ye clergy ye would derogate from ye honour and
dignity of your family, whereas, in strict reasoning, the contrary thereof would appear, and yᵗ it would very much tend to
support the honour and dignity of it. Of this I hope you will
be better convinced when you consider the titles of honour

and respect that are given to those who are invested with ye
ministerial functions, as are amply displayed in ye Scriptures.
Those invested with that character are called the ministers of
Christ, ye stewards of the mysteries of God, to whom they
have committed the word of reconciliation—ye glory of Christ,
ambassadors of Christ in Christ's stead, co-workers with Him,
Angels of the churches. And then it is moreover declared that
whosoever despiseth them despiseth not man, but God. All
which titles shew that upon many accounts they stand called,
appropriated to God himself. And therefore, if a gentleman
of this sacred and honorable character should be married to
a lady, though of ye greatest extraction and most excellent
personal qualities (which I am sensible you are endowed with),
it can be no disgrace to her nor her family, nor draw ye censures of ye world upon them, for such an action. And, therefore, dear Madam, your argument being refuted, you can no
longer consistently refuse to consummate my happiness.

JOHN THOMPSON.

May, 1742.

A reconciliation was effected between Mr. Thompson and Mrs. Spotswood's family some years afterwards, by the kind offices of that remarkable man,
Rev. R. Rose, who was one of Governor Spotswood's
executors, and had much to do with his estate, and
with his widow and children after Governor Spotswood's death, which happened in 1740, at Annapolis,
on his way to command the army against Carthagena. Mr. Rose, in his journal, speaks of having
visited Mr. Thompson in Culpeper, as he seems to
have done every other man of note in the colony.
Mr. Rose's journal, a great desideratum to antiqua-
ries, and which was supposed to have been lost, was
seen by Bishop Meade in the possession of Mr. Henry
Carter, of Caroline, and is now in the possession of
Mr. Brock, of Richmond.*

*Since writing the above I have been permitted by the kindness of Mr.
Brock to make the following extract from Mr. Rose's journal:

The next few years are rather barren of known incidents. The following small items from the parish register serve to fill the gap. (1741) Goodrich Lightfoot came into the vestry, took the oath of allegiance, signed the test, and subscribed to be conformed to the doctrine and discipline of the Church of England, in the place of Thomas Stanton, deceased. (1742) Ordered, that notice be given in church and chapel that a vestry will meet first Monday in March, to place a church convenient to the inhabitants of the upper part of the parish, and that workmen come and agree for building the same. At a vestry held in Tenant's old field, a contract was made with J. Kincaid to build a church fifty-eight feet by twenty-four. Benjamin Roberts is chosen vestryman in place of Captain William Triplett, removed. Robert Slaughter places a dial at the church door. (1743) Vestry contracted with J. Eve for an addition to Little Fork Church. (1744) "Ordered, that the Rev. J. Thompson erect, fabricate, and build (*sic*) divers additions to the Glebe house." William Peyton is directed to view the church three times. (1745) Captain Abraham Field chosen vestryman, in place of F. Kirtley, removed, and Philip Clayton in place of John Catlett, deceased. (1746) B. Roberts and Coleman Brown are lay readers at the two churches, James Pendleton at the chapel, and Thomas Dillard

"1746, Feb. 18, I set out for Germanna, called at Capt. Taliaferro's, lodged at Newport.

"19th, went in the rain towards Germanna; met Mrs. Spotswood Dandridge and Isaac Campbell, who waited for us at the Bridge quarter; got to Germanna at night. 20th, spent in settling sundry accounts. 21st, went at night to Major Finlason's. 22d, went to church, heard Mr. Thompson preach on the words, "Your life is hid with Christ in God;" went to the Glebe. 23d, settled I hope all differences in the family, and laid a plan for preventing any. 24th, came early to Germanna, where found Col. B. Moore and his lady; settled Mr. Thompson's account with some others. 26th, went from Newport to see Mr. Benger's plantation."

at the Little Fork. (1747) Robert Slaughter vestryman, in place of Major Finlason, deceased. Dr.
James Gibbs is paid " for doing his best to cure the
widow George." (1748) At this date Orange was
divided, and the county of Culpeper (comprising
what is now Madison, Rappahannock and Culpeper)
was formed. It was named after one of the proprie-
tors of the Northern Neck, Lord Culpeper, from
whom it descended to Lord Fairfax, who married
his daughter. The original county of Culpeper covered all the "debatable land" between the Crown
of England and Lord Fairfax east of the Blue Ridge,
and was for a long time the subject of a very curious
controversy, a synopsis of which will be found in the
next chapter.

CULPEPER COUNTY.

1748. Culpeper county begins its career on historical ground. Its territory originally embracing what
is now Culpeper, Madison and Rappahannock, was
the subject of a protracted controversy, involving
the title to several million acres of land. The entire
tract of land " within the heads of the rivers Tappahannock, alias Rappahannock, and Quiriough, or
Potomac, the courses of those rivers, and the Bay of
Chesapayork, &c.," was granted at different times, by
Kings Charles I. and II., to Lord Hopton, the Earl of
St. Albans, and others, and subsequently by King
James to Lord Culpeper, who had purchased the rights
of the other parties. Lord Fairfax, who married the
daughter of Lord Culpeper, became the proprietor of
this princely domain, commonly known as the Northern Neck. In 1705 Governor Nott, of Virginia,

in the name of the King, granted 1920 acres of
land to Henry Beverly, in the forks of the North
and South branches of the Rappahannock River.
Robert Carter, commonly known as King Carter,
who was Fairfax's agent, objected to the grant, as
being within the limits of Lord Fairfax's grant. The
question then arose whether the South (the Rapidan)
or the North branch of the Rappahannock was the
chief stream. The Rapidan, named after the English
Queen, contested the supremacy of the Indian Rappahannock. The Governor and Council of Virginia
appointed commissioners to meet those of Fairfax,
and survey the said rivers. The joint commission
reported in 1706 that the streams seemed to be of
equal magnitude. In 1733 Lord Fairfax complained
to the King that patents had been granted, in the
name of the Crown, in the disputed territory. Mr.
Carter himself, the agent of Fairfax, had taken
grants from the Crown to two tracts within the forks
of the Rappahannock River. The King, in council,
ordered the Governor of Virginia to appoint another
commission. On the part of the Crown he appointed
William Byrd, of Westover, John Robinson, of Piscat-
away, Essex county, and John Grymes, of Brandon,
Middlesex county, Virginia. The commissioners of
Fairfax were Charles Carter, William Berkley and
William Fairfax. Omitting the survey of the Potomac, as outside of our subject, we confine ourselves
to the survey of the Rapidan. Mr. Graeme, with Mr.
Hume as assistant, was commissioned on the part of
the Crown, and Mr. Thomas on the part of Lord
Fairfax, " to survey and measure the South Branch
of the Rappahannock (the Rapidan), from the fork
to the head spring, and return an exact map of the

same, describing all the runs and creeks that run into it." Colonel Byrd says :—" While we stayed at Fredericksburg we lodged at Colonel Henry Willis's, but kept a magnificent table at the ordinary, and entertained all gentlemen who came to visit us, which were many. We then went to the fork of the river, and found the North branch to be wider by three poles and nine links, though it was objected by my Lord's Commissioners that the South was made narrower by an island that ran along the south shore. We carried a surloin of beef from Colonel Carter's, and picked it as clean as a pack of wolves would those of a wounded deer. The same gentleman furnished us with strong beer, but forgot to bring a vessel to drink it from. However, we supplied that want with the shell of a poor terrapin, which we destroyed, as Henry VIII. did Cardinal Wolsey, for the sake of his house. We then proceeded to Germantown, where Governor Spotswood received us very courteously, and lest we should have forgotten the battles of Marlborough, he fought them all over again, for the nine-and-fortieth time. There we took the depositions of Taliaferro, Thornton, and Russell, as follows :—Jno. Taliaferro, gentleman, aged forty-nine years, being summoned, saith :—' About the year 1707 he came to live where he now lives, above Snow Creek, nine miles below the falls, and there were then but three settlements above his house, on the south side of the river. He had been acquainted with the fork of the river above twenty-four years, and that one of the forks was called South River until Governor Spotswood, above twenty years ago, named the south branch Rapidan, and it has ever since been so called.' Francis Thornton, of Caro-

c

line, gentleman, aged fifty-three years and upwards, being sworn, declared:—'About thirty years ago he came to dwell where he now lives, on the lower side of Snow Creek, and there were but two settlements above his house, the uppermost of which was about four miles below the Falls. He had been acquainted with the forks of the river about twenty-seven years, and that one was called the South and the other the North Branch.' William Russell, aged fifty-six years, being sworn, saith:—'He has known the Great Fork of the Rappahannock River thirty-five years as a hunter, and one of the branches was always called South River until he heard Governor Spotswood named South River Rapidan, and the other river has been called Rappahannock; that the uppermost settlement thirty years ago was Montjoy's tobacco-house, now Colonel Carter's quarter, on the north side of the river; that he saw some posts of the house on Mott's land, three or four miles above the Falls, which was said to have been burned by the Indians near thirty years ago."

On the 3d August, 1736, the King's Commissioners met at Williamsburg. Major Mayo attended with an elegant map, delineating clearly the branches of the Rappahannock up to their sources, and with copies of their field-notes. The commissioners of the King made their report. Lord Fairfax took the report of his commissioners to England with him, and got the matter referred to the Lords of Trade, to report all the facts and their opinion to the Lords of the Committee of Council. All the reports and papers were laid before the latter. The question was argued by able counsel; and without going into further details, let it suffice to say, that it was finally decided in

favor of Lord Fairfax; making that branch of the
Rapidan, called the Conway, the head-stream of the
Rappahannock River, and the southern boundary
of the Northern Neck; and thus adding the original
county of Culpeper to the princely plantation of
Lord Fairfax. The Rapidan, named after an
English Queen, prevailed over the Indian Rappahannock. Queen Ann's name and reign are perpetuated
in Rapidan, North and South Anna, Fluvanna,

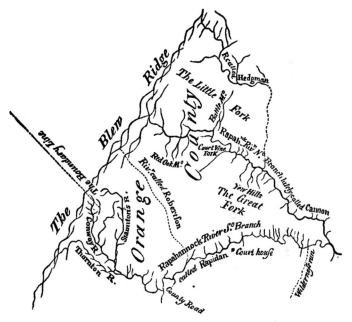

Rivanna, Germanna, &c. Authorities differ as to
the orthography of the name of the river in question.
Many spell it Rapid Ann; and yet in the proceed-
ings of the commissioners for settling the boundaries of the Northern Neck, and throughout Henning's
Statutes at large, it always has the form Rapiddan
or Rapidan. The decision referred to was ratified
by the formal assent of the General Assembly, and
by the authority of the highest judicial tribunals.

1749. William Green is chosen vestryman in the place of Capt. Robert Green, deceased. The county of Culpeper was now honored by the presence and services of George Washington in the humble office of County Surveyor. The marriage of his brother Lawrence with Miss Fairfax made him known to the proprietor of the Northern Neck, who gave him the appointment of Surveyor. In 1748 he was employed in the valley of the Shenandoah. His compensation was a doubloon ($7.20) a day. In the following year he was made a public surveyor by the President of William and Mary College ; and in the County Court of Culpeper we find the following record :

July 20th, 1749. "George Washington, gentleman, produced a commission from the President of William and Mary College, appointing him Surveyor of this county, which was received ; and thereupon took the usual oaths to his Majesty's person and government ; and took and subscribed the abjuration oath and test, and then took the oath of surveyor, according to law."

Washington was now in his seventeenth year, and continued in office for three years. As no one had the sagacity to see the undeveloped germs of greatness which lay hid in this unfledged youth, his daily life passed without special observation. Had it been otherwise, we should in all probability have found, in our old parish register, the record that he was the surveyor who laid off our glebes and sites of churches, and ran some of our parish lines.

1750. A "chapel of ease" was ordered at the Little Fork, and the vestry agreed to meet at or near

A

BOOK OF SURVEY'S

Began

JULY 22$^\text{d}$. 1749

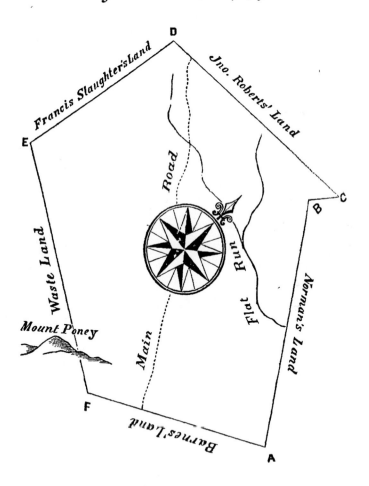

the old muster-field at the forks of the road, to choose
the site, and contract with Thomas Brown to under-
take it.

1751. Thomas Slaughter is chosen vestryman in
place of Robert Slaughter, Jr., removed from the
parish; and James Pendleton in place of Capt. Ball,
deceased. Gabriel Jones is paid 200 pounds tobacco
for attorney's fees, Dr. Thomas Howison 1000
pounds tobacco for medical attendance on the poor,
and Wm. Peyton 200 pounds tobacco for procession-
ing lands.

1752. St. Mark's Parish is again divided by the
Meander or Crooked Run, falling into the Robinson
River, up to Col. John Spotswood's corner on that
run, thence by his line, north 28 degrees east to
Bloodsworth's road, then by a straight line to Crooked
Run, a branch of the north fork of the Gourdvine
River, where the main road called Duncan's crosses
the said run, thence by the said run up to the head
thereof; thence to the head of White Oak Run,
thence by that run down to the North River. All
below that line, except so much as lies in the county
of Orange, to be one distinct parish, and retain the
name of St. Mark's; and all above said bounds, together with so much of St. Thomas as lies in Culpeper,
which is hereby added to and made part of the same,
be another distinct parish and called Bromfield (see
6th Henning 256). As this division threw Tennant's
Church into the Parish of Bromfield, the church
wardens were ordered to provide benches or seats in
the court-house for the accommodation of so much of
that congregation as remained in St. Mark's. This
gives the date of the first church services held at
Culpeper Courthouse. The churchwardens were

also ordered to apply to the surveyor to run the lines between the parishes, and Henry Field and Philip Clayton were directed to attend the surveyor when running these lines. Mr. Brown was also ordered to remove the materials for the intended chapel in the Little Fork, and to erect a church, instead of a chapel, with them, on a ridge between Freeman's* Mill Run and the river, in the edge of Freeman's old field — the church to be ceiled with plank instead of clapboards, and to have wainscot instead of plain pews, in the best manner. A new church was also ordered upon Col. Spotswood's land, near the cool spring above John Leavell's, on or near Buck Run. The present writer well remembers to have seen, in his boyhood, the relics of the burying-ground of this old church, which stood in a grove upon the hill, above and across Buck Run from the dwelling where old Capt. Moore then resided, and Capt. John Strother now lives.

1753 to 1757. Some of the leaves of the vestry book have been torn out, leaving a gap in the record from 1753 to 1757, which Bishop Meade has passed over. I propose to fill that gap from the folio, which is entire, and with inevitable inferences from other known facts. One of these inferences is, that there was a church at Mount Poney. The ground of this inference is the fact that an appropriation had been made for a church at that place in 1752; and one of Mr. Thompson's manuscript sermons (still extant) is

---

* This Freeman was the grandfather of Mrs. Waller Yager. His father and Major Eastham came from Gloucester county, and were among the early settlers in what is now Culpeper. Mrs. Yager's father was one of the first members of Little Fork Church. His father owned a large body of land there. He died in the 96th year of his age, leaving five sons and four daughters.

endorsed as having been preached at Mount Poney Church some years after.

The names of the following persons appear in a record before me as having served in a campaign against the French and Indians about this date, viz: Col. Robert Slaughter, Lieut.-Col. Wm. Russell, Capt. Wm. Brown, Capt. John Strother, Lieut. John Field, Lieut. William Slaughter, Martin Nalle, Wm. Nalle, Charles Yancey, Wm. Lightfoot, Reuben Long, Thomas Slaughter, William Robertson, Wm. Yager, Henry Gaines, Henry Stringfellow, and Wm. Roberts. All these names have their representatives still in Culpeper, and they are reproduced as items of interest to their descendants. Robert Slaughter, Robert Coleman, Daniel Brown, Philip Rootes, Reuben Long, and Wm. Williams, are spoken of as being neighbors. Dr. Michael Wallace presented an account to the vestry for 800 pounds of tobacco, for curing Eliza Maddox. Daniel Brown, James Spillman, and Henry Field, are credited with services rendered; and C. Hutchins is allowed 100 pounds of tobacco for grubbing the churchyard at Little Fork.

1757. The vestry met at the vestry-house, and the following gentlemen were present:—Rev. Mr. Thompson, minister; Wm. Lightfoot, Robert Green, Goodrich Lightfoot, Wm. Green, James Pendleton, Francis Slaughter, Robert Slaughter, Philip Clayton, Benj. Roberts, and Henry Field. James Pendleton was continued as Clerk (Lay Reader) of Little Fork Church; Nat. Pendleton, Clerk of the Lower Church; Richard Young, Clerk of Buck Run Church, and Wm. Peyton, Clerk of the Vestry. The church-wardens were directed to provide two new surplices

and two prayer-books for the use of the parish. Col.
Wm. Green and Col. Wm. Russell were made churchwardens for the ensuing year, and Robert Eastham
vestryman, in place of Thomas Stubblefield, deceased.
Divers poor and infirm persons were exempted from
paying parish levy, and appropriations were made
for the support of all poor and disabled people. Last
Monday in November, 1757, vestry met at the new
church on Buck Run. H. Field reported that he had
paid the quit-rents for the glebe and church for 1755-
56. Thomas Covington was paid for tarring the
church, grubbing the yard, and making the horse-block
at Buck Run.

1758. Dec. 1st, Robert Eastham and Robert
Green churchwardens for the ensuing year. Thos.
Slaughter and Anthony Garnett made vestrymen, in
place of Wm. Stubblefield, deceased, and Wm. Lightfoot, removed out of the parish. James Pendleton,
Sheriff, gave bond and security as collector of parish
levy.

1759. In February, Act of the General Assembly
established the town of Fairfax, on a "high and
pleasant situation in the county of Culpeper, where
the courthouse now stands"; and set apart thirty
acres of Robert Coleman's land, to be laid off into
lots and streets by the trustees, Thomas Slaughter,
Wm. Green, Philip Clayton, Nat Pendleton, and
Wm. Williams. This land was held by Benjamin
Davis, lessee of Coleman, who was permitted to hold
his houses, and have one-fifth of his rent deducted.
Hence the names of Davis and Coleman Streets.
Nov. 26th, 1759, payments were made to William
Russell, R. D. Parks, J. M. Tackett, Charles Morgan,
and J. Carnager, R. Wright and Joseph Newman,

for providing for certain poor persons. Thomas Slaughter and Anthony Garnett made churchwardens for ensuing year.

1760. Robert Slaughter and Francis Slaughter appointed churchwardens for 1761, and James Slaughter collector. The wardens are instructed to provide any number of benches that may be needed, to stand in and about the Little Fork Church. This order would seem to indicate that the congregations of Mr. Thompson were too large to be accommodated in the regular seats. Wm. Williams is chosen vestryman in place of Robert Eastham, removed out of the parish.

1761. Sept. 1st, an addition to Little Fork Church, 32 feet long and 22 feet wide, was ordered. Thos. Covington, with Lewis Davis Yancey as his security, gave his bond to build it for 100 pounds. Nov. 1761, the usual annual appropriations for the poor were made. 1500 pounds tobacco were ordered to be sold out of the depositum for cash, to pay 100 pounds to Covington for additions to Little Fork Church. Goodrich Lightfoot and William Williams were chosen churchwardens for the ensuing year, and John Green collector.

1762. Sept. 1st, Wm. Pollard was elected clerk of the Lower Church. An order of Bromfield Parish being exhibited by Ambrose Powell and Martin Nalle, gentlemen of the vestry of said parish, to join them in the division of the two parishes, it is ordered that the same lie for the further consideration of the vestry. From this entry it would seem that although the two parishes had been separated for ten years, the parish lines had not been run. Dec. 18th, 1762, at a vestry at Little Fork Church the

usual routine business was gone through, and Henry
Field and Benjamin Roberts made churchwardens
for the ensuing year.

1763. April 8th, Wm. Ball was chosen vestryman
in the room of James Pendleton, deceased, and
Henry Field, Jr., in the place of Henry Field, Sr.,
resigned. Philip Clayton was chosen to succeed
Henry Field as churchwarden.

Dec. 19th, "Wm. Ball, and Henry Field, Jr.,
having in the court of Culpeper taken the oath
to his Majesty, and subscribed the test, and in the
vestry subscribed to be conformable to the doctrine
and discipline of the Church of England as by law
established, took their places as vestrymen accordingly." The above entry is more circumstantial than
usual, but it only describes in detail what always
took place when a new vestryman was qualified.
Wm. Ball and Henry Field made churchwardens
for the ensuing year. 5500 lbs. of tobacco were set
apart for repairing the Lower Church, and 3000 lbs.
for paying allowances to the poor.

1764. Nov. 19th, appropriated to Thos. Covington, in full satisfaction for repairing the church,
vestry-house, dial-post, stand and six benches, 700
lbs. of tobacco, he having already received 3500 lbs.

The Rev. Mr. Thompson having represented to
the vestry that the glebe-land of this parish is in-
sufficient to furnish timber, fire-wood and fences, the
vestry do order that a petition be presented to the
General Assembly for an act enabling the vestry to
sell the glebe and purchase another in lieu thereof.
Mr. Thompson having asked for leave to build a
gallery in Lower Church for the use of his family, the
vestry consent, provided the lower part of the gallery

be above the windows and not inconvenient to any part of the church, except the back pew, in which the stairs are to be carried up. John Green and Robert Green are appointed churchwardens.

1765. Nov. 26th, the usual routine business being dispatched, the vestry adjourned to meet at Frederick Zimmerman's on the 17th Dec.

Dec. 17th, ordered, that the churchwardens agree with workmen to build a house at Buck Run Church, and another at the Fork Church, each 12 feet wide and 16 feet long, well framed and covered with shingles free from sap, weather-boarded with feather-edged plank, underpinned with brick or stone 18 inches from the surface of the earth, a brick or stone chimney to each, sash windows to each with eight lights of glass 8 by 10 inches, with a plank floor above and below. We give the style of these houses in detail because they are specimens of the vestry-houses of that day, and illustrate some other points. James Slaughter and James Pendleton were elected vestrymen in the room of Francis Slaughter, gentleman, deceased, and Thos. Slaughter, who had removed from the parish. Goodrich Lightfoot and William Williams church wardens for next year.

1766. Nov. 17th, Samuel Clayton chosen vestryman in room of Major Philip Clayton. Benjamin Roberts and James Pendleton made churchwardens for next year, and appropriations for current expenses.

1767. Nov. 24th, James Slaughter and Samuel Clayton churchwardens. Samuel Clayton, Jr., in behalf of the congregation of Buck Run Church, moved that R. Young be removed from being Reader at said church, and said Young is ordered to answer the complaint on the 18th of December. Mr. Young soon after came into the vestry and resigned. The cause of complaint is not stated.

1768. February 23d, an addition to Buck Run Church twenty-eight feet wide and three feet long, sills, sleepers, posts and braces all of oak, and underpinned with brick or stone, is ordered; and Captain William Brown being the lowest bidder at 11,500 lbs. of tobacco, it is let to him upon his entering into bond with security that it be done in a workmanlike manner, and finished by October of the ensuing year.

November 23d, James Pendleton and G. Lightfoot churchwardens for the ensuing year, and Cadwallader Slaughter appointed vestryman in the place of Robert Slaughter, deceased.

1770. Leave is given to Samuel Henning to build a gallery in Buck Run Church at his own expense. The wardens are instructed to advertise the glebe for sale in the Virginia Gazette, and to buy a more convenient site for a glebe. The glebe was sold to Samuel Henning for one hundred and ninety-nine pounds current money. Goodrich Lightfoot and others reported that they had viewed several tracts of land, and that Francis Slaughter's or George Catlett's was the most convenient for a glebe. The vestry adjourned to meet at Lawrence Catlett's and decide upon the site. John Green vestryman in the room of William Green, deceased.

November, the vestry this day bought three hundred acres of the tract on which Francis Slaughter lives (Francis Slaughter owned a large tract of land, including the old glebe tract, near what is now

D

called Brandy Station), and adjoining the lands of
Reuben Slaughter and Cadwallader Slaughter, gentlemen, for 199 pounds in money and 10,000 pounds of
tobacco.   An overseer's house, a quarter, a barn and
a corn-house are ordered to be built on the glebe
immediately.

1771. At a vestry at Buck Run Church, French
Strother, gentleman, and John Gray, gentleman, are
made vestrymen, in place of Goodrich Lightfoot and
Henry Field, gentlemen, removed from the parish.
Philip Pendleton is made clerk of the vestry in
place of William Peyton, deceased.   Mr. Peyton had
served the vestry as clerk for forty years continu-
ously.   An addition is ordered to the south side of
Little Fork Church, to correspond to the other addition.   These enlargements of the church, new gal-
leries and extra benches, would seem to show that Mr.
Thompson's ministry was attended by large and
growing congregations.   Mr. Waugh chosen a vestryman in 1772.   Colonel James Slaughter, gentleman,
agreed to have the glebe-house built for 35,900
pounds of tobacco.   The plans and specifications are
minutely detailed in the vestry-book.   This was the
glebe-house so long occupied by the reverend and
venerable John Woodville, and afterwards by Messrs.
Glassell and Wager.   The original glebe-house was
burned ; perhaps some of the outbuildings may be
standing.

The glebe-house, the plan of which is described in
the last chapter, was built for the Rev. John Thompson ; but man proposes and God disposes.   Before
this earthly tabernacle was finished, Mr. Thompson
was called to "a house not made with hands, eternal

in the heavens." After a laborious and fruitful ministry of more than thirty years, the brave soldier of the Cross laid aside his armor and put on his crown. He was buried at the brick house near Stevensburg so long tenanted by the Hansbroughs, and now owned and occupied by Dr. Grayson. By his first wife (Lady Spotswood) he had two children, viz: Anne, who in her fifteenth year married Francis Thornton of Fall Hill, near Fredericksburg. Mr. Thompson had also a son by Mrs. Spotswood, named William, who married Miss Sally Carter of Cleve. Among their descendants were Commodore Thompson of the U. S. Navy, and many of the Thompsons of Kentucky.

After the death of his first wife, the Rev. John Thompson married Miss Rootes. One of their children was the Hon. Philip Rootes Thompson, who once represented the district of Fauquier and Culpeper in Congress, and then moved to the county of Kanhawa, where his family was the nucleus around which was gathered the Episcopal Church and Parish at the mouth of Coal, one of the tributaries of the Kanhawa River.

The second wife of the Hon. P. R. Thompson was a daughter of the old patriarchal vestryman, Robert Slaughter of Culpeper. Bishop Meade said of her, "She was esteemed and loved by all who knew her, as one of the humblest and most devoted members of the church in Virginia. I have always (he adds) felt my own sense of the Divine power and excellency of religion strengthened by every visit to her abode. She exchanged it some years since for a better one above."

After the death of Mr. Thompson, the Rev. Charles

Woodmason was employed to do some service in the parish. This is all that seems to have been known by our historians of this person; but I have found in " Perry's Collection," a memorial to the Bishop of London signed by him, in which he says:—" Through much sickness, brought on by fatigue in traversing the back part of Carolina, I had accepted for my health the Parish of Bromfield in Culpeper county. Being delayed so long in waiting for a successor, Bromfield was granted away, fearing its lapse to the Governor, while I was on my way. I might have gotten some other parish, had not the Virginians entered into resolves *not to elect any man for their minister but a native of America.*" This explains the whole matter, and shows the patriotic spirit of the vestry of St. Mark's, among whom were some persons who soon became conspicuous in the war of the Revolution. November, 1772, the vestry proceeded to consider of a proper person to recommend to the Governor as minister of the parish, when the Rev. Edward Jones, of Carolina, was unanimously nominated. James Slaughter and John Gray were chosen churchwardens. January 6th, 1773, the Rev. Edw. Jones produced his induction from the Governor, appointing him minister of this parish, agreeable to a presentation of a former vestry, and took his seat in vestry accordingly. April 21st, 1773, the vestry met to fix on a site for the mansion on the glebe, and finding no place where water was convenient, agreed with Mr. Francis Slaughter for 100 acres of land adjoining the former purchase, for the sum of £150 current money. October 26th, 1773, the church in the Little Fork having been burned, the vestry met on the ground, and concluded to erect one of wood, sixty feet long and forty feet wide, on Robert Free-

man's or Peter Bowman's land. It was also ordered
that William Williams, John Green, James Slaughter,
and Cadwallader Slaughter have James Pendleton's
tobacco-house repaired for Divine worship until the
church be finished. December, 1773, the vestry
reconsidered their former order and resolved to build
a church of brick, eighty feet long and thirty feet
wide in the clear, with twenty feet pitch, to be
finished completely in the best manner by first day
of November, 1776. Thirty thousand pounds of
tobacco to be paid next summer, and the balance to
be paid in three equal annual payments.

This is the old brick church in the Little Fork
which has stood for *one hundred years*, the mute
memorial of other times and other men. The walls
of this centennial church once resounded with the
voices of sires, some of whose sons now pass by on
the other side, or look coldly at the shrine where
their fathers worshipped, and speak lightly of the
anthems they sung in days of auld lang syne.

> And rudely sighs the wandering wind,
>   Where oft, in years gone by,
> Prayer rose from many hearts to Him,
>   The Highest of the High.
> The tramp of many a busy foot
>   That sought thy aisles is o'er,
> And many a weary heart around
>   Is stilled forever more.

> Oh! could we call the many back
>   Who've gathered here in vain,
> Who careless roved where we do now,
>   Who'll never meet again,
> How would our souls be stirred
>   To meet the earnest gaze
> Of the lovely and the beautiful,—
>   The light of other days.

The churchwardens are ordered to let the following buildings on the glebe-land, viz.:—A kitchen thirty-two by sixteen feet, with an inside brick chimney with two fire-places, covered with good shingles and boarded with feather-edged plank. A quarter twenty by sixteen feet, covered with long shingles, and boarded with good oak-boards, and an inside wooden chimney. Also, a dairy and meat-house twelve feet square, each to be done in the best manner; a stable twenty feet square, of sawed logs, covered with long shingles; also, seven hundred feet of sawed paling, five feet long, with sawed rails three square. The wardens are also ordered to let the building of a gallery in the Lower Church. John Green and James Pendleton are ordered to agree with Peter Bowman for two other acres of his land, for the use of the church.

1774. Benjamin Roberts and John Green are appointed churchwardens for the ensuing year.

1775. The vestry met to lay the parish levy, but the inspecting law ceasing, they are in doubt what method will be pursued through this colony for levying and collecting the same, and concluded to await the opinion of the General Convention.

1776. The vestry met and proceeded to lay the levy. Robert Gaines was made the clerk of the Lower Church, in place of John Hume. It is ordered that Peter Bowman be paid two pounds for one and a half acres of land for the use of the brick church, and that Edmund Vass be paid five pounds for two plans for the brick church. The collector is ordered to pay Samuel Clayton three pounds seven shillings and sixpence for laying off the brick church lot, and Mr. Ball and James Pendleton are made churchwardens for the ensuing year. Richard Yancey is chosen vestryman in the place of John Green, *in Continental service.* (This is the only allusion to the Revolutionary War in the vestry-book. The vestry seem to have limited themselves rigidly to their duties, and never to have invaded the political sphere, although several of them were officers of the army, and all sympathized with the American cause. Culpeper county was conspicuous for the services of her sons in the old Revolution, having contributed eight companies of eighty-four men each to the army. Those companies were raised by the following captains, viz.: John Green, John Thornton, George Slaughter, Gabriel Long, Gabriel Jones, John Gillison, Captain McClanahan (a Baptist preacher), and Abraham Buford. In the notes and illustrations at the end of this volume will be found some interesting details upon this point. We return to the acts of the vestry.)

1777. Ordered, that the churchwardens advertise the vacancy of this parish and the renting of the glebe. As Mr. Jones had not resigned, this looks like a broad hint that his resignation would be accepted.

1778. The General Assembly having suspended the salaries of clergymen, the vestry met to fix on some method of paying the salaries of the officers of the church, and recommended subscriptions for that purpose. The recommendation is signed by French Strother, James Slaughter, William Gray, Robert Green, Robert Yancey, Benjamin Roberts, Cad. Slaughter and James Pendleton. Burkett Davenport is made vestryman in place of Wm. Williams, deceased.

1780. February 21st, the Rev. Edward Jones this day came into the vestry and resigned the charge of this parish. In March the vestry met at Captain Bradley's, and ordered that the Sheriff collect of each tithe in the parish five pounds tobacco, or in money at the rate of twenty-five per hundred. Robert Pollard and Lawrence Slaughter are appointed vestrymen to fill the vacancies. In the ensuing April the vestry met at the glebe, and agreed to receive the Rev. James Stevenson as minister of their parish, according to law, and Thomas Stanton was made lay-reader at the Little Fork Church, in the room of Philip Pendleton, resigned. The vestry met again in December of this year, and ordered certain payments to be made to John Jameson, clerk of the county, Henry Field, Reuben Long, Robert Latham, William Terrill, and Michael Sloane, for the benefit of the poor of the parish. Lawrence Slaughter and Robert Pollard churchwardens for the ensuing year.

1781. Robert Coleman made collector, and ordered to collect of 1957 tithes seven pounds of tobacco each, for the clothing, feeding, and providing medical attention for the poor distributed among the farmers.

1782. Ordered, that the churchwardens inform the poor claimants of this parish three months before meeting that they attend the vestry (if able) and let their situation be known.

1783. Bowles Armstead appointed vestryman in the room of Benjamin Roberts, deceased.

1784. Resolved, That the churchwardens provide the goods for the poor on the best terms they can and report the result. James Jett is appointed clerk of the vestry, and Samuel Clayton and Robert Yancy churchwardens.

This is the last meeting of the vestry recorded in
the old register, which began in 1730. This gap in
the record of the parish can only be filled with a
general outline of its history, which must be gathered from many scattered sources. Rev. James
Stevenson probably continued to be the minister of
St. Mark's Parish until he exchanged places with
Mr. Woodville, the former going to Fredericksburg
and the latter coming to Culpeper.

THE ORGANIZATION OF THE CHURCH IN VIRGINIA.

1785. The Episcopal Church in Virginia had its
first legislative council. For 175 years it had been in
bondage to the Crown and Parliament of Great
Britain. For political reasons it was not allowed
to have a Bishop, nor to make a law for its own
government, or for the discipline of its ministers and
members. One of its first acts after becoming free,
was to meet in convention and frame a constitution
and code of discipline. Mr. Stevenson, with James
Pendleton, lay deputy, represented St. Mark's in
the Convention of 1785. One of the first acts of the
Church, when free, was to divide the State into
districts, the ministers in each district forming a
"Presbytery." To supply, in some measure, the
place of a Bishop, a clergyman was appointed to
visit each district and to preside in its presbytery.
Mr. Stevenson was made visitor of the district composed of the parishes of St. Mark's, St. George's,
Bromfield, and Berkley. In 1786 St. Mark's was
represented only by Robert Slaughter, lay delegate.
Mr. Stevenson was the minister of Berkley Parish,

Spotsylvania, in the interval between 1768, when
he was licensed for Virginia, and 1780, when he took
charge of St. Mark's Parish. Col. Taylor, of Orange,
in his diary of 1787, says:—"I went to James
Taylor's to the marriage of Thomas Barbour and
Jane Taylor by the *Rev. James Stevenson*," and in
1788 he says:—"Thomas Barbour's son was baptized and named James Taylor."

In January, 1794, he was elected by the unanimous
vote of the people assembled at the market-house in
Fredericksburg. It was during his charge of St.
George's that those two institutions which have
done so much good, the male and female charity
schools, were instituted.

In 1799 Mr. Stevenson preached the annual
sermon in behalf of these schools, whose pupils
were required to go to church and be catechised by
the minister, for which the teachers were bound to
prepare them. In 1802 he preached an appropriate
discourse on the anniversary of St. John the Evan-
gelist, before the Masons of Fredericksburg. Soon
afterwards he was confined by a protracted illness in
Culpeper, from which he never sufficiently recovered
to resume his ministry. The following correspondence will explain the occasion of his resignation:

FREDERICKSBURG, *July 25th*, 1805.
DEAR SIR:
In conformity to a resolution of the trustees of your church,
at a meeting on the 24th inst., we beg leave to express the
just sense entertained of your past services, and the sincere
regret that your indisposition has so long deprived us of their
continuance. It has been intimated that you had expressed
yourself doubtful of your health's enabling you to perform
those clerical duties, so justly appreciated; though from
motives of personal consideration, the trustees feel a repug-

nance in the discharge of this duty, yet the welfare of this church requiring every attention that can promote it, and well knowing your unremitting zeal for its interest, we flatter ourselves that you will excuse the request we now make, of being informed of your intention of continuing in the office of your present appointment.

With sentiments of affectionate regard, we are, very respectfully, dear sir, your obedient servants,

WILLIAM TAYLOR,
JAMES BROWN,
Church Wardens.

[*Answer.*]

CULPEPER, *July* 29*th*, 1805.

GENTLEMEN:

Your letter of the 25th current came to hand yesterday; and I am requested by my husband to make his acknowledgments for the sentiments therein contained, both in regard to his past services and health. As to the latter, he has but little hope of its being established so far as to enable him to perform the duties of a parish; but he begs you will believe, that the zeal he has hitherto manifested towards your church is still alive, and to hear of its welfare will ever be grateful to him. He therefore recommends it to the trustees to provide a minister as soon as they can, and that he may be one every way suitable is his sincere wish.

With much respect and esteem, I am, gentlemen, yours, &c.,

FRANCES STEVENSON.

Mr. Stevenson married Miss Littlepage, a lady of fine intelligence and culture. The Hon. Andrew Stevenson, who was Speaker of the House of Representatives and Minister to England, and the late Carter Stevenson, were his sons. The Hon. J. White Stevenson, late Governor, and present Senator in Congress from Kentucky, is his grandson. Mr. Stevenson survived his resignation of St. George's several years, and departed this life June, 1809. The following brief item from the *Virginia Argus*

furnishes the only intelligence we have of the event:
"Died on Friday in Culpeper, after a tedious illness,
the Rev. James Stevenson, a gentleman much and
deservedly esteemed by an extensive acquaintance."

Since the foregoing pages were written we have
received from Dr. Payne, of Tennessee, some valuable
illustrations of the lives of his grandfather Woodville
and his great-grandfather Stevenson. Of the latter
he says he was an invalid in his last days, having
been stricken by paralysis, and was the guest of
Mr. Woodville at St. Mark's glebe. Your father, he
adds, Capt. P. Slaughter, was one of his vestrymen,
and gave me many interesting incidents of his
private life. His last family residence was Hopewell,
near Fredericksburg, where the Hopewell nursery
now is. His library was bought for a mere trifle by
a gentleman of Fauquier, who designed returning it
to the family, but died before fulfilling his purpose.
The following is a copy of his letters of ordination
(now before us), engrossed on parchment:

Be it known unto all men by these presents, that we,
Richard, by Divine permission, Bishop of London, holding by
the assistance of Almighty God a special ordination on Thurs-
day, 29th of September, in the year of our Lord 1768, being
the feast of St. Michael the Archangel, in the chapel of our
Palace in Fulham in Middlesex, did admit our beloved in
Christ, James Stevenson, (of whose virtuous and pious life and
conversation, and competent knowledge and learning in the
Holy Scriptures, we were well assured) into the Holy Order of
Priests, according to the manner and form prescribed and
used by the Church of England; and him, the said James
Stevenson, did then and there rightly and canonically ordain
a Priest. He having first in our presence and in the form of
law taken the oaths appointed by law to be taken for and instead of the oath of supremacy, and he likewise having freely
and voluntarily subscribed to the 39 articles of religion, and to
the three articles, contained in the 36th canon.

In testimony whereof, we have caused our Episcopal seal to be hereunto affixed. Dated the day and the year above written, and in the fifth year of our translation.

MARK HOLMAN,

LONDON. *Dep. Reg.*

On the mitred seal appended is inscribed the seal of Richard Terrick, Bishop of London, 1764.

Among the documents sent by Dr. Payne is an original Thanksgiving sermon preached by Mr. Stevenson at Mattapony Church, Berkley Parish, Spotsylvania, on Thursday, 13th of November, 1777, on the occasion of the surrender of Burgoyne's army. In outward form the sermon is a curious relic of by-gone days. It is about four inches long and six inches wide. It consists of nineteen pages, with only nine lines on each page. In point of sentiment and literary execution it is excellent, and gives us a pleasing illustration of the piety and patriotism of one of our old colonial ministers.

REV. JOHN WOODVILLE.

In the progress of our narrative we have reached in Mr. Woodville a link between the two centuries, overlapping several generations. There are those now living who remember his antique face and form. Patriarchs who were once his pupils still linger on the horizon. Many survive upon whose brows he poured the waters of holy baptism; some whom he visited in sickness, and to whom he administered the holy communion; and there are hundreds for whose fathers and mothers, grandfathers and grandmothers, he performed all these offices, consigning them at last to the tomb in the burning words of our grand old

E

burial-service. His official advisers, those venerable
vestrymen, Robert Slaughter, of "The Grange";
Peter Hansbrough, of "Coal Hill"; Champ Carter,
of "Farley"; John Jameson, Clerk of the County;
William Broadus; Samuel Slaughter, of "Western
View"; John Thom, of "Berry Hill"; Isaac and Walter Winston, of Auburn, with whom he took counsel
and walked to the house of God in company, are all
gone. The parish register, in which were recorded his
official acts, and which, like the old register we have
been following, would have been such a fruitful
source of information for the illustration of the history
of the parish and county, cannot be found. We are
therefore limited to the few facts scattered through
the extant journals, and the memories of living men,
for materials to construct a meagre skeleton of his
administration.

Mr. Woodville having been a teacher, with a board-
ing school under his charge, could not always attend
the conventions, which were held in Richmond, the
horse being almost the only mode of locomotion in
those days. Mr. Woodville, who married a daughter of
the Rev. James Stevenson, succeeded him as minister
of St. Mark's. Mr. Woodville, like Mr. Stevenson,
was elected minister of St. George's Parish by a vote
of the people assembled in the market-house in
Fredericksburg. The vote was ninety-six for Mr.
Woodville and thirty-four for Rev. Thomas Davis,
whereupon Mr. Woodville was proclaimed by the
senior warden, Mr. Day, to be duly elected. In the
Virginia Herald of that date we find two brief notices
of him. In June, 1792, he preached a well-adapted
discourse before the Masons. In a poem of the day,
written by a minister apologizing for levity of

conversation with which he had been reproached, occur these lines :

> "Deny him not those aids within his reach ;
> But let me laugh, and modest Woodville preach."

Mr. Woodville was Professor of the Humanities in the Fredericksburg Academy when Gilbert Harrow was Professor of Mathematics. These gentlemen were required to be examined by Bishop Madison in the classics and in the sciences. It is probable that Mr. Woodville spent some years in teaching before he was chosen as minister of St. George's Parish, as I find in the diary of Colonel Frank Taylor, of Orange, under the date of 1789, the following entry : " Mr. Woodville preached to a large congregation on Sunday at Orange C. H., and he preached to a much larger one on the Sunday before at Pine Stake Church, near Raccoon Ford."

In 1791 St. Mark's was represented in Convention by David Jameson as lay delegate; in 1796 by Mr. Woodville and Robert Slaughter; in 1797 by J. Woodville and John Jameson; in 1805 by William Broadus; in 1812 by J. Woodville and Robert Slaughter; in 1814 by William Broadus. The Convention appointed Robert Slaughter, Peter Hansbrough and Garland Thompson to collect funds in Culpeper for the resuscitation of the church. In 1815 J. Woodville represented St. Mark's Parish, and the Rev. William Hawley and Samuel Slaughter represented St. Stephen's Church, which is the first appearance of the latter upon the record.

And now a new era begins to dawn on the Church in Virginia. The black cloud of despair is spanned by the bow of hope. The good providence of God sent Bishop Moore to lead the "forlorn hope," and never was there a man better fitted for the special crisis. Baptized with the Holy Ghost and with fire, his heart was a gushing spring of emotion, which overflowed his eyes, and streaming from his eloquent tongue and trembling hands, melted his hearers to tears. He wept over the ruins of the old churches and the scattered sheep without a shepherd, like the lamentation of Jeremiah over the desolation of Zion.

In St. Mark's Parish the first fruit of this new movement was St. Stephen's Church, at Culpeper C. H., and its first heralds were the Rev. Wm. Hawley and Mr. Samuel Slaughter, all making their first appearance on the record in 1815. There is no record that I can find of the building or consecration of St. Stephen's Church. It connects itself with history at this point, but when and how it came into being has eluded all my researches in print and in the memories of living men.

Bishop Moore reported having visited Culpeper during the past year, and confirmed sixty persons. This was the first and the largest confirmation ever held in the parish. In August of this year Bishop Moore preached in four places in Culpeper, and confirmed eighteen. He also reports having ordained Mr. Hawley to the priesthood. Mr. Hawley was elected a delegate to the General Convention. He extended his labors to Orange C. H., and after a ministry of two years he was called to St. John's Church, Washington, where he spent the remainder of his days, beloved by all men. Of his ministry in Culpeper and Orange, Bishop Meade said he "preached and labored with much effect." And Rev. Mr. Earnest, in his sketch of St. Thomas,

Orange, says :—When Mr. Hawley began his labors
in Orange the Episcopal Church had wellnigh died
out. But three or four communicants remained.
Under his ministry there began to dawn a brighter
day for the Church. Some of the communicants
added by him still remain. During Mr. Hawley's
administration Bishop Moore made his first Episcopal
visit to Orange, and preached with great effect, and
administered the rite of confirmation to a goodly
number. It was the first confirmation ever held in
St. Thomas's Parish. Among the goodly number was
the aged mother of President Madison, who had
never before had an opportunity of ratifying her
baptismal vows. The ministry of Rev. Mr. Hawley
was evidently blessed in this parish ; but having
been called to a larger field, he took charge of St.
John's Church, Washington, which soon became a
centre of much influence. In the course of Mr.
Hawley's ministry there he numbered among his
parishioners many Presidents of the United States,
and other persons of the highest social and political
position, before whom he went in and out for more
than a quarter of a century, "an Israelite indeed in
whom is no guile." He was among the originators
and most earnest supporters of our Education
Society, and of the measures which led to the establishment of our Theological Seminary. Of the
tributes to his memory by Dr. Tyng and others, one
of the most loving was by the Rev. Dr. Lawrie, of
the Presbyterian Church, between whom and Mr.
Hawley there prevailed an intimacy like that between
Bishop Johns and Dr. Hodge, of Princeton, and
between the Episcopal Buchannon and the Presbyterian Blair, of Richmond. When the prayers for

the sick were read at the bedside of Mr. Buchannon,
he said, with childlike simplicity, "Pray for Blair,
too." There is an anecdote of Mr. Hawley among
the traditions current in Culpeper which, whether
true or not, is too good to be lost. The story is that
Mr. Hawley wore ruffles on his shirt-bosom, as was
common among gentlemen of that day, and that
some ladies asked him to have them removed, as
they were thought not becoming a clergyman. To
this he gracefully assented. But he wore whiskers
also, and was told that these were an offence to the
weak brethren. To this he is said to have replied,
with a gleam of mischievous good-humor playing on
his face, "Oh no! ladies. I must keep my whiskers
to save my ears."

In 1817 St. Mark's Parish was represented by the
Rev. Mr. Woodville and Wm. Broadus, and St.
Stephen's Church by Samuel Slaughter and Isaac
Winston. In 1818, the same lay delegates, St.
Stephens is reported without a minister, notwithstanding most strenuous efforts to get one. In 1819
St. Mark's was represented by Col. John Thom, who
reported twenty-five baptisms, four marriages, nine
funerals, and forty-five communicants, five of whom
were additions since the last convention. In 1820
the Rev. Herbert Marshall came to Culpeper and
took charge of the school at Capt. Philip Slaughter's,
of which John Robertson, the father of Judge Robertson of Charlottesville, and the Rev. Samuel Hoge,
father of Dr. Moses Hoge of Richmond, had been
masters. Mr. Marshall was ordained Priest by
Bishop Moore at Walker's Church in Albemarle,
and officiated very acceptably for several years as
pastor of St. Stephen's Church. His name only

occurs in 1822 in the Journals of the convention, with Wm. M. Thompson, father of present Secretary of the Navy, as lay delegate. His wife was the sister of the present venerable presiding Bishop. His brief and promising ministry was cut short by ill-health and a premature death. He, like Mr. Hawley, officiated at Orange C. H.

Mr. Woodville continued his modest ministry as rector of St. Mark's, officiating chiefly at the Lower Church and at the Little Fork, and occasionally at Stevensburg and the Courthouse; but St. Stephen's Church seems to have been in a state of suspended animation, until it was revived by the coming of the Rev. G. A. Smith in 1826. Mr. Smith having been in charge of Christ Church, Norfolk, and finding it too heavy a burden for his delicate health, came to rusticate and to renew his strength in this Piedmont parish. His name appears in the convention journal as representing, with Samuel Slaughter, St. Stephen's Church, and with Peter Hansbrough as delegate from St. Mark's Parish in 1827. From that time till 1830 Mr. Smith officiated alternately at St. Stephen's Church and at Orange C. H., with occasional ministrations at Stevensburg and elsewhere. He established a Bible class, and societies in aid of mission and other Church charities. He gave an onward impetus to the church, reporting an accession of nine members by confirmation in 1828; and Bishop Meade reports eleven confirmations in 1830, when Mr. Smith, from physical infirmities, resigned his charge, an event deeply deplored in the report of the lay delegate, Dr. Winston, to the next convention.

Mr. Smith is one of those mysterious instances, so

trying to our faith, of a man thoroughly furnished for the work of the ministry, and with an eye so single to the glory of God, and yet, for the want of organs through which to reveal the light that is in him, has passed much of his life in the shade, comparatively unknown and unsung, while men of far feebler powers and scantier furniture, but with stronger physique and more self-assertion, have worn the mitre and wielded the sceptre of influence. But he has not lived in vain. As editor of the Episcopal Recorder and of the Southern Churchman, and master of the school at Clarens, he has made his mark and will leave his impression upon many minds. He still lives, the patriarch of our alumni, and the fitting president of their society. May Providence prolong his years, that though his voice be hushed, the graces of his daily life, like angels trumpet-tongued, may plead the cause he loved so well. In this brief tribute I have departed from a rule laid down by Bishop Meade, and which I have prescribed to myself, not to sound the praises of living men, leaving that to those who may come after them and see their end. But as the case is unique, this single exception must prove the rule; which, by the way, Bishop Meade did not always follow himself.

In 1831-32, Isaac Winston and P. Slaughter, Jr., represented St. Stephen's Church. Mr. Woodville, though not present, reported St. Mark's Parish as gradually improving, the congregations as visibly increasing, and there being in many persons a greater anxiety to encourage "pure and undefiled religion." In June, 1832, the Rev. A. H. Lamon took charge of St. Stephen's Church in connection with

Madison C. H.; and in 1833 he reported an accession
of eight communicants to St. Stephen's, and twenty-
four at Madison, to the six whom he found there.
In reference to the revival at Madison, Bishop Meade
said :—" We had services four times a day for three
days. It was a joyful season for the church at
Madison. Fifteen months before, I scarcely knew a
place which promised less to the labors of a minister
of our church. At this visit I confirmed twenty-
three warm-hearted disciples of Christ, and saw a
new brick edifice rising for their place of worship.
God had signally blessed the preaching of his word
by ministers of different denominations. He had sent
to our communion an humble and faithful man, who,
going from house to house, in season and out of
season, was the instrument of gathering an interesting little band, with whom I spent some of the
happiest days of my ministry. I also admitted their
minister Mr. Lamon to Priest's orders."

In 1834 Mr. Lamon reports the addition of eight
persons to the communion of St. Stephen's, the
establishment of a scholarship in the seminary, and
measures for the purchase of a parsonage, and the
permanent establishment of a minister among them.
Bishop Meade, in his report of 1834, said :—" On the
4th September, 1834, I preached to a large congregation, and confirmed eight persons at the Little
Fork in Culpeper. The congregation was then, and
had been for a long time, under the care of the Rev.
Mr. Woodville. At this place he most conscientiously
and patiently met with his people for many years;
here had I often met him in my travels during the
last twenty-two years, and here it was that I saw him
on the occasion just mentioned for the last time. Pro-

vidence has removed him from a scene of sincere obedience on earth to one of glorious enjoyment in heaven. He has left an affectionate family to mourn the loss of a kind husband and tender father, and many friends to cherish, with sincere respect, the memory of a conscientious Christian." Such was the tribute of the evangelical Wm. Meade to the child-like John Woodville, and it does as much honor to the author as it does to the subject of his praise. It is too common in these days of cant to disparage these old-time Christians, because their religion was not in our style. Such censures are as irrational as it would be to find fault with an antique statue because it is not arrayed in modern fashionable costume, or to disparage St. James because he did not give the same prominence to the doctrine of justification by faith as did St. Paul, but presented chiefly the moral phase of the Gospel — there being, in truth, no more incongruity between the doctrines and the morals of Christianity than there is between the root of a tree and its fruit.

Mr. Woodville left a son, the Rev. J. Walker Woodville, who for some years followed in the footsteps of his father. He was a good and guileless man. His other son, James, was a lawyer in Botetourt, and Woodville Parish perpetuates the name. Of his wife and daughters, Fanny and Sarah, Bishop Meade said, "I do not expect to meet purer spirits on this side of heaven." These sainted women, I learn from their relative, Senator Stevenson, of Kentucky, both died in Columbus, Mississippi. Dr. J. W. Payne, a prominent citizen of Tennessee, a grandson of Rev. John Woodville, and a great-grandson of the Rev. Mr. Stevenson, is probably the owner of the

family relics and traditionary mementoes of his
ancestors of St. Mark's. Mr. Woodville was buried
at Fredericksburg, with the service of the church
and of his brother Masons, on the 10th of May, 1834.
He desired, says Dr. Hugh Hamilton, to be laid near
the body of Mr. Littlepage.

Dr. Payne has also furnished me with some very
pleasant reminiscences of his grandfather Woodville,
and enables me to supply what was wanting in the
foregoing sketch of Mr. Woodville. Dr. Payne was
born at St. Mark's glebe, and educated and fitted
for college by his grandfather. In his boyhood he
used to attend him in his visitations, "carrying the
communion service in his saddle-bags," after the
death of Mr. Woodville's body-servant, "Uncle Jim."
He speaks plaintively of the old churches in the
Little Fork and Big Fork (Lower Church.) Of the
latter he says it was a plain structure of wood.
The gallery (called Lady Spotswood's gallery) was
in ruins. The only thing of taste about the church
was a marble baptismal font, the gift, he thinks, of
Mrs. Spotswood, and the monument of Mr. Downman. He had seen the communion administered by
Mr. Woodville to old Mr. Robert Slaughter and
old "Uncle Jim," and perhaps sometimes to one
other servant belonging to some Episcopal family.
On such occasions he sometimes omitted the sermon,
but never a word of the service. Of the old brick
church in the Little Fork, he says the long, square,
high-backed pews, the sounding-board, the pulpit,
reading desk and clerk's stand, its transverse aisles,
its chancel in the east, the Lord's Prayer and Ten
Commandments elegantly painted upon the communion table, carried you back to a past generation.

The congregations here were generally large; and there were many Episcopal families in the neighborhood—Gen. M. Green, the Porters, Picketts, Farishes, Wiggintons, Freemans, Spilmans, Withers, Paynes, &c. But you had to see it filled, when the Bishops came, to conceive what it was in days of old. "I hope," he adds, "it was spared during the war, for I saw at that time in the newspapers that a sermon was found beneath the pulpit, preached near fifty years ago by Mr. Woodville, 'whose classic elegance,' &c., surprised its captors."

From the same authority we learn that Mr. Woodville was born at White Haven, Cumberland County, England, in 1763, came to America in 1787, lived as tutor in the family of Rev. J. Stevenson, who sent him with commendatory credentials, and a letter from the Rev. Mr. Scott, Principal of St. Beno School, and testimonials countersigned by the Bishop of Chester, to Bishop White, who ordained him Deacon on the 18th, and Priest on the 25th of May, 1788, in Christ's Church, Philadelphia. He took charge of the Academy in Fredericksburg in 1791, and of the church in 1792, became Rector of St. Mark's in 1794, and spent the remainder of his life at the glebe. He was a great sufferer in his last years from dropsy of the chest, but never murmured. He spoke of his death with perfect composure, saying that his only reliance for salvation was upon the merits and righteousness of Christ; often saying in his last illness, *I die happy.* His last words were "God bless you all." (See obituary in Episcopal Recorder, January 25th, 1834.)

On the fly-leaf of his wife's devotional manual are the following lines:

His mind was of no common order, and under the immediate and habitual influence of the strongest religious prin-
ciples; such was my dear and ever-lamented husband.

GLEBE, *March 8th*, 1834.   SARAH WOODVILLE.

The following is the inscription on his tombstone :
"Underneath, the body of John Woodville, a true
believer in the Holy Scriptures, an earnest minister
of the Protestant Episcopal Church, a diligent and
faithful teacher of youth, a meek, contented sojourner
on earth, a pious probationer and humble candidate
for heaven. In Anglia natus die Martii undecimo
MDCCLXIII; obiit Virginia undecimo die Januarii
MDCCCXXXIV."

His wife, Mrs. S. S. Woodville, died at Buchanan,
Va., April 6th, 1848, calm in mind and pure in
heart, meekly resigned to the will of heaven, at
peace with God, and in charity with all the world.

Thus lived and died the last Rector of St. Mark's
Parish. Other churches, with other pastors, had
sprung up and flourished within his cure. He bade
them all "God speed"; but we note that in his private
diary he called them all chapels.

Among the many early pupils of Mr. Woodville
were the Hon. Andrew Stevenson and the Rev.
George Hatley Norton, Sr. Of the latter, Mrs.
Woodville was often heard to say, "He was the
best boy ever in the school." He was a Virginian,
but lived most of his life, and died in Geneva, New
York. He was the father of Dr. Norton, the great
church-worker of Louisville, Kentucky, and of Dr.
George H. Norton, the able and efficient Rector of
St. Paul's Church, Alexandria.

F

REV. JOHN COLE.

Mr. Cole was born in Wilmington, Delaware. He conceived the idea of studying for the ministry in 1822, and after concluding his course in the Theological Seminary of Virginia, was ordained by Bishop Moore, in Petersburg, on the 18th of May, 1828. He preached his first sermon at the Lower Church, in Surry county, Virginia, on the 23d of May of the same year. He spent the first two years of his ministry in missionary work in Surry and Prince George, endeavoring to revive the fires upon the altars of the old churches, which had nearly gone out. From a diary of his ministry I infer that he was diligent in preaching the Gospel in the pulpit and from house to house, in establishing Sunday schools, and such like good works. He preached his last sermon in this county January 16, 1830, at Cabin Point. Soon afterwards he took charge of Abingdon and Ware Parishes, in the county of Gloucester, where he ministered usefully until 1836, when, with a view of seeking a more bracing climate, he resigned his charge.

The author of this history, being then rector of Christ Church, Georgetown, D. C., was visited by Mr. Cole, and advised him of the vacancy of St. Stephen's Church, Culpeper. I being about to go to Culpeper to solemnize several marriages, introduced Mr. Cole to the people of St. Stephen's, by whom he was invited to fill the vacancy. He accepted the invitation, and took charge of St. Stephen's in conjunction with two churches in Madison county. In 1838 he made his first report on his new field of labor, reporting at St. Stephen's thirty female and five male communicants, at Madison Courthouse twelve communicants, and at Trinity twelve. Of the last he says quaintly :—"This church is significantly called a free church, which, in country parlance, means free to everybody and everything, for winter and summer, snow and storm, heat and cold." His services, he adds, in these parishes, including Stanardsville, are twelve sermons a month, besides a Bible class, a lecture, and prayer meetings weekly. Rev. J. Walker Woodville, in the same year, reported seventeen communicants of St. Mark's Parish.

In 1840 Mr. Cole resigned the churches in Madison to Rev. Mr. Brown, and took charge of the new congregation of St. James, Culpeper. In 1841 the St. James congregation applied for admission into the Convention. The Convention reported against the application, as not being in conformity with the requisitions of the canon. The report was recommitted to an enlarged committee, and Dr. Winston and Dr. Hamilton came before them and testified that "St. Mark's for several years had not been in an organized state, but had gone into decay, and that the canon could not be complied with." Upon this testimony St. James was admitted as a separate congregation. Mr. Cole reported thirty communicants at St. Stephen's and eleven at St. James, with a neat and comfortable church ready for consecration. In 1842 St. James was reported as having been consecrated by Bishop Meade, who had also confirmed twelve persons. The communion at St. Stephen's, after rising to fifty-three in 1845, fell to thirty-one in 1847; while at St. James it rose from fifteen in 1843 to twenty-seven in 1848. In 1849 Rev. Walker Woodville reports St. Mark's with regular services at Little Fork, Flat Run, and the Germanna woollen factory, which probably were the only Episcopal services at Germanna for one hundred years. In 1850 Mr. Cole reports the completion of the "Lime Church" (St. Paul's), at a cost of only about $1000.

In 1859 Mr. Cole resigned St. James Church, that it might be united with a new church in Fauquier. In 1850 the communicants at St. Stephen's had risen to fifty-three, and those at St. Paul's to twenty-seven. In 1860 R. H. Cunningham, lay delegate, represented St. James, and reported a parsonage as being in progress there. In July of the same year Mr. Mortimer, a student at the seminary, began lay reading at St. James. S. S. Bradford represented St. Stephen's and P. P. Nalle St. Paul's, which latter applied for admission into the Convention as a separate congregation for the third time, as they allege. Mr. D. Conrad, for the committee, questioned the constitutionality of establishing separate congregations in one parish, with power to elect lay delegates, as destroying the equilibrium between the clergy and laity in Convention; but having been assured by Mr. C. and the petitioners that the congregation is desirous of being admitted as a parish, and intended so to make application, the committee recommend that the said separate and petitioning congregation be admitted as a parish, to be called St. Paul's Parish, in the county of Culpeper, according to the boundaries set forth in said petition. This report does not seem to have been voted upon, and is not found in the record; yet in 1861 Mr. Cole reports St. Paul's Church *in St. Paul's Parish.* In 1862–3 there were no Conventions. In 1864 none of the

Culpeper churches were represented. In 1865 Mr. Cole reports St. Stephen's and St. Paul's churches in *St. Mark's Parish.* In 1866 St. Paul's is reported as having been destroyed ; but in 1868, the last year of Mr. Cole's life, he again reports St. Paul's Church in *St. Paul's Parish,* as having been rebuilt by the generosity of a Virginian by birth (Mr. John T. Farish), but residing in New York. The new St. Paul's was consecrated by Bishop Whittle Nov. 8th, 1868. It is impossible now to unravel this tangled skein of facts. In 1869 there is no report, and in 1870 St. Paul's Church reappears in *St. Mark's Parish,* and we hear no more of *St. Paul's Parish.*

But we have anticipated the chronological order of our narrative, and must return to 1861, when Mr. Mortimer reports St. James Church, St. Mark's Parish, with twenty-eight communicants and the contribution of $3000 for a parsonage. Mr. Cole reports in the same year the enlargement of St. Stephen's church-edifice, with a steeple of fine proportions, and a fine-toned bell, at a cost of $2500, nearly the whole of which was raised within the congregation.

And now the " war-clouds rolling dun " over-shadowed the land. The peaceful parish became an intrenched camp, and a highway for the marching and counter-marching of grand armies. The churches, so lately resonant with anthems of praise, are torn down or converted into barracks and hospitals and stables, and the roar of artillery and the blast of the bugle supercede the songs of the sanctuary. Mr. Cole in his report of 1865-66, tells the tale with bleeding heart and bated breath. He says : " Since my last report of 1861, cruel war has raged. Pen cannot write nor words utter the trials of mind and heart, and the privations endured. All the Episcopal churches in this county, and every other place of worship within the lines of the Federal army (except the Baptist and Episcopal churches at the Court-house), were utterly destroyed by it during the winter of 1863-64. The whole country is a wide-spread desolation. The people, peeled and poor, are strug-gling for a living. During the occupation by the Federal army we were not permitted to use our church. We worshipped God, like the primitive Christians, in private houses, and never did the ser-vices of the Church seem sweeter or more comforting. I visited the sick and wounded, and buried the dead of both armies alike — the number of funerals being 490. It is a record for the great day, and not for the Convention. There were twenty churches of different denominations destroyed within a comparatively small area. Among these in this parish were St. Paul's and St. James, and Calvary Church, under the care of Rev. P. Slaughter, at the foot of Slaughter's (Cedar) Mountain. The last named church was built by Mr. Slaughter on his own place when by ill-health he was constrained to retire to the country. This church was consecrated by Bishop Johns in June, 1860, and Mr. S. officiated for the benefit of his neigh-bors and servants, without fee or reward, other than that arising from the consciousness of trying to do some good, under the burden of many infirmities. The only relic of this church is a beautiful stained window, which was spared at the intercession of a young lady, who kept it under her bed till the war was over. That window now lights a chancel in Mr. Slaughter's dwelling, which also contains a desk, the

only relic of another of his old churches which was
burned. The chancel, with its relics, has in it the
seeds of an unwritten poem, whose melody is only
heard in the heart."

Mr. Slaughter, in his report to the Convention in
1865, says:—" Since the destruction of my church
and the desecration of my home by Federal soldiers,
I have spent my time in the army and in the hospitals, and in editing the 'Army and Navy Messenger,'
a religious journal for our soldiers and sailors." The
despoiled church at Culpeper has been restored by
the aid of friends; St. Paul's has been rebuilt by the
kindness of Mr. Farish; St. James has risen from the
ashes at the bidding of Miss Wheatley and others;
but a few stones and a little grove of evergreens of
second growth are all that mark the spot where once
stood a consecrated fane at the foot of Slaughter's
Mountain. The wailing winds play requiems upon
the evergreen harps of pine, and the birds singing
sweetly among the branches, with responsive echoes,
are now the only choir which chants anthems, where
once young men and maidens, old men and children,
praised the name of the Lord. It is proper to say
that Mr. Slaughter has declined contributions for
rebuilding this church, in favor of other churches
where the field promised a better harvest.

Whether this church shall rise again God only
knows. His will be done! If a sparrow cannot fall
to the ground without his notice, much less can a
church perish by violence. If it rise not, then let
the wailing winds still play its requiem, and the plain-
tive dove chant its funeral dirge.

After officiating on Christmas day, 1868, Mr. Cole
was stricken by paralysis, and in a few days finished

his career of forty years' service in the ministry,
thirty-two of which were spent in St. Mark's Parish.
Dr. Dalrymple, in his address at the Semi-Centenary
of the Seminary, calls special attention to our obligations to Mr. Cole for his successful labors in adding
to our emolument fund, and for his agency in pro-
curing the charter for our Theological Seminary.
He also records the following interesting incident,
which we had heard from Mr. Cole's own lips:—At
a convention many years ago, when the clergy and
laity were assembled around the chancel at the close
of the services on Sunday night, Bishop Moore called
on Mr. Cole to raise a hymn.   He obeyed by commencing:

> The voice of free grace
> Cries, escape to the mountain.

It was caught up by Bishop, priest and people, singing
jubilant at that solemn hour of night.   Such was the
origin of this time-honored custom of the Convention
of Virginia.

Rev. Mr. Cole married first, April 10th, 1855,
Fanny E., daughter of John Thompson of Culpeper
— children, Fanny Meade, John Thompson, Thomas
Willoughby and Carter Stanard; and married, second,
Mrs. Conway, daughter of Wm. Foushee.   His second
wife soon followed her husband to the tomb, dying
without issue.

After what has been already said, Mr. Cole may
be characterized in a few words.   In all the relations
of life he was a true man, transparent as Dryden's
ideal man, whose thoughts were as visible as the
figured hours through the crystal of a clock.   He
was not what is called a popular preacher (a ques-

tionable compliment, since it too often implies the arts of the demagogue), and he had a true English hatred of all shams. He was a faithful and brave soldier of the Cross, not ashamed of the faith of Christ crucified, but manfully fought under his banner unto his life's end. A fitting inscription upon his tomb would be these words: "He feared God — he had no other fear."

THE SUCCESSORS OF THE REV. MR. COLE.

Having now taken leave of the dead past, we stand in the presence of the living. We must be wary of our words, not only because (as Dr. Hawks said of Bishop Moore in his lifetime) we would not "shock the delicacy of living worth"; but because it will be the office of those who come after them and see their end, to mark their place in history. The only exception to this rule we have already noted, he having no more active field-work to do.

The Rev. George W. Peterkin, who had been assisting his father at Richmond, took charge of St. Stephen's Church in June, 1869. In 1870 he reported an addition of 26 to the communion of 1868, which he found there at his coming. Sunday School more than doubled; sermons and addresses during the year 140, and 40 public catechisings. The Rev. Chas. Yancey Steptoe, who had been recently ordained, and had recently taken charge of Christ and St. Paul's churches, reported an accession of 18 to the communion, with 110 Sunday school teachers and scholars. Bishop Johns, in 1869, had consecrated Christ's Church, " which (he said) from its position supplied the place of two churches destroyed during the war. For this beautiful building we are indebted to the Christian sympathy of Miss E. A. Wheatley, formerly of Culpeper, now of Brooklyn, New York. She provided the funds and furnished the plan. It stands in full view of the railroad, a pleasing memorial of the pious devotion of a lady who loved her people and built them a Christian synagogue."

In 1871 Mr. Peterkin reported a handsome brick building at a cost of $1669.40, raised on the credit of the vestry, and the organization of a church school for girls, under the charge of Mr. K. S. Nelson. Mr. Steptoe reports an addition of 21 to the communion of Christ and St. Paul's churches, and a contribution of $1215.23. In 1872 Mr. Peterkin reports an addition of 44 to the communion of St. Stephen's, a Sunday school of 200, and 3 teachers and 27 scholars in church school. " During the past year (he says) the school has sustained itself, and become a recognized power in the parish. An important part of my work (he adds) during two years past, has been the restoration of an old colonial church, about twelve miles from Culpeper, in the Little Fork. $250 have been spent in necessary repairs, of which $100 was from the Bruce Fund. Congregations large, and 8 communicants at the old church." Mr. Steptoe reports the building of a rectory near Brandy Station for the use of Christ and St. Paul's churches, at a cost of $2150, of which Christ's Church contributes $1005; St. Paul's, $450; Piedmont Convocation, $180; Miss Wheatley, $415, and Mr. Suter, of New York, $100. A steeple, bell, and other improvements have been added to Christ Church by our kind friend Miss Wheatley. In 1873 Mr. Peterkin reports 137 communicants, a Sunday school of 280, of whom

35 are colored children, 3 teachers and 39 scholars in the church school, which, he says, is so established and governed as to enable the church to extend the blessing of Christian education among her people. Mr. Steptoe reports a church at Rapidan Station as nearly finished by our own efforts and the aid of friendly communicants at Christ and St. Paul's churches.

1874. Rev. James G. Minnegerode having succeeded Mr. Peterkin (who had taken charge of Memorial Church, Baltimore,) reports 145 communicants and a Sunday school of 282. Mr. Steptoe, for Christ, St. Paul's, and Emmanuel churches, reports 96 communicants and Sunday schools of 86, contributions $1545.11, the consecration of Emmanuel Church by Bishop Johns on the 10th of December, 1873. "I officiated (he says) at Emmanuel's two Sundays in the month, in the afternoon, until we were so fortunate as to secure the services of the Rev. Dr. Slaughter, as long as his health shall hold out. By the aid of Mr. J. Wilmer, Jr., as Lay Reader, he has been able to officiate on Sunday mornings." Dr. Slaughter himself says he has been much aided by the sympathy and co-operation of Mr. Steptoe and of the Bishop of Louisiana, who spends some of the summer months here, and is always ready to help us with good words and good works.

1876. PRESENT STATUS OF THE CHURCHES IN ST. MARK'S PARISH.

St. Stephen's Church, Rev. J. G. Minnegerode, Rector:—Communicants 170, Sunday school teachers and scholars 200, of whom 50 are colored.

Christ and St. Paul's Churches, Rev. C. Y. Steptoe, Rector:— Communicants, after subtracting those transferred, 80.

The present writer officiates at Emmanuel Church. Of his work there it does not become him to speak, except to say, that he deems it a privilege at this eleventh hour of his ministry to be permitted to do even a day's work in the vineyard. Communicants 36, the number having just trebled since the institution of regular services.

At the last Convention St. Mark's was again divided, and Ridley Parish taken out of its eastern side, by a line beginning at Jameson's Mill, on Muddy Run, with that Run to Hazel (Eastham's) River, thence with that river to the Rappahannock River, with Rappahannock to the mouth of the Rapidan, up the Rapidan to the mouth of the Robinson, up the Robinson to Crooked Run, up that run to Wayland's Mill, thence to the top of Mount Poney, thence to the beginning. The new parish includes Christ's, St. Paul's, and Emmanuel churches, and leaves to the now mutilated St. Mark's only St. Stephen's Church at Culpeper, and the old Centennial Brick Church in the Little Fork, the only representative in this parish of the Church of England in the "Colony and Dominion" of Virginia.

We have said in the text that we had not been able to fix the precise date of the building of St. Stephen's Church, Culpeper C. H. General Edward Stevens (the Revolutionary hero), who lived in the house now occupied by Mrs. Lightfoot, in his will, recorded in August, 1820, "confirms his promise to give one acre of land in Fairfax" for an Episcopal church, one acre adjoining the village for a Presbyterian church, and one acre to Free Masons' Lodge of Fairfax adjoining his family burying-ground for a cemetery. St. Stephen's was built between 1820 and 1823.

ST. THOMAS PARISH, ORANGE COUNTY.

This parish was cut off from St. Mark's in 1740, carrying James Barbour and Benjamin Cave, vestrymen, along with it. Before the separation St. Mark's had built a church, since known as the Old Orange Church, near Ruckersville, and a chapel where Robert Brooken now lives. There was also a chapel ordered at Bradley's or Batley's quarter, whose site was to have been fixed by Benjamin Cave. After the separation, St. Thomas' vestry built the Pine Stake Church, near Raccoon Ford, on land originally patented by Francis Taliaferro; and a middle church below Orange C. H., on land now owned by Erasmus Taylor. All trace of the Pine Stake Church is gone. The writer remembers in his boyhood to have been at a barbecue at the church spring. The middle church was of brick, and was well preserved as late as 1806. Some years later it shared the fate of many other old churches, which were assumed to be common property, and were torn down and carried off piece by piece. The gilt altar-piece, with other ornaments of the chancel, were attached to household furniture. The old communion service, engraved with the name of the parish, given by the grandmother of President Madison and other good women, has been recovered and is now in use.

Unhappily the old records of St. Thomas Parish have been lost, so that it is no longer possible to

G

reproduce the chief early actors in it. The Rev.
Mungo Marshall was minister in 1753. There was
once a tombstone over his grave, but that too was
appropriated, and was used in a tannery to dress
hides upon. In 1760 he was succeeded by the Rev.
Wm. Giberne. In 1761 the Rev. James Marye followed, and his first official act was the funeral sermon
of the paternal grandmother of President Madison.
In the family record it is said, "her funeral sermon
was preached by Rev. J. Marye, jr., from Rev. 14
ch. 13 verse." In 1767-8 the Rev. Thomas Martin
succeeded. He was a tutor of President Madison, and
lived for a time in the family at Montpelier. He
was a brother of Governor Martin of North Carolina.
A letter from Mr. Madison to him expressing a great
respect and affection for his preceptor, may be seen
in "Reves' Life and Times of Madison." Rev. John
Burnett succeeded Martin about 1770, and was followed by Rev. Jno. Wingate, the last of the colonial
clergy, who being suspected of want of loyalty to
Virginia, soon took his leave. The disloyal odor this
man left behind him may have been the reason why
the vestry, who were very patriotic (James Madison,
the vestryman, was chairman of the Orange committee), did not have another minister for twenty-three
years, contenting themselves with occasional services
by the Rev. Matthew Maury of Albemarle. The old
churchwarden, Major Moore, buried the dead with
the church service, and the Rev. Mr. Belmaine, while
paying his court to Miss Lucy Taylor, and on his
visits after his marriage, officiated. The Rev. Henry
Fry (Methodist) was sometimes called upon to
preach, always preceding his sermons with the old
church service (says Col. Frank Taylor in his

diary.) In 1780 the vestry engaged the blind Presbyterian minister Mr. Waddell (whose eloquence has been so glorified and transfigured by the genius of Mr. Wirt) to officiate for them once a month in the Brick (Middle) Church, and gave him 60 pounds. Mr. O'Neil was the minister from 1790 to about 1800. In 1809–11 the Rev. Hugh C. Boggs officiated at Orange C. H. and the Pine Stake Church, which was standing as late as 1813.

This brings us to the time when the minister from Culpeper began services in Orange, of which an account will be found in the body of this work. The church at Orange C. H. is modern, having been built in 1833-34. The history of the services of the Messrs. Jones, Earnest, Davis, Carson, and Hansbrough, are within the knowledge of those now living, and need not be reproduced here; it not being within the scope of this book to give more than a brief sketch of Bromfield and St. Thomas, as having been originally within the bounds of St. Mark's Parish.

Col. Frank Taylor's diary enables one to form a life-like conception of the animated social circle of which Orange C. H. was the centre from 1786 to 1799. The circle embraced Montpelier, Coleman's Springs, Clarke's Mountain, and parts of Culpeper and Madison counties. The persons who figured in it were Col. Frank Taylor, James Taylor (Clerk of the County), Dr. Ch. Taylor, the family physician, and Erasmus, Robert, John, and other Taylors, whose name is legion. Col. Thomas Barbour and his brother James, James Barbour, Jr., Dr. Thomas Barbour, Richard Barbour—Ambrose, Gabriel, Philip, son of Thomas; Philip, son of Ambrose; and another Philip Barbour. Major Moore, Robert, John, and

William Moore, and many more. Col. James Madison, Sr., Col. James, Jr. (President), Ambrose, William, Ca tlett, and other Madisons. Crump, Charles, Ben, and Abner Porter. William and R. B. Morton, A ndrew Shepherd, Sr. and Jr., and John and Alexander Shepherd. A whole chime of Bells — John, William, Thomas, and Charles. Col. Lawrence, Hay, Frank, and William Taliaferro. Capt. Catlett, Frank, Jo hn Catlett, Jr., and Henry Conway. Col. James Pendleton, Nat., Henry, John, Bowie, Philip, and countless other Pendletons, chiefly from Culpeper. Capt. William and Francis Dade. Andrew and John Glassell, Reuben Smith, James and John Walker. Z achary, Robert, and John Burnley, and Isaac and John Williams, and Samuel Slaughter. Divers Alcockes, Lees, and Gibsons, &c., &c. Among the young ladies were Lucy, Sally, and Fanny Barbour; Nancy, Sally, Betsy, Patsy, Lucy, and Polly Taylor; Franky Alexander, Milly and Polly Glassell, Hannah Watkins, Lucy Gaines; Mary, Betsy, Sally, and Suky Conway; Fanny, Elizabeth, Joanna, and two Katies Pendleton; Sally, Betsy, and Judy Burnley; Sally, Nelly, Elizabeth, and Frances Madison; Fanny and Polly Moore, the Misses Gilbert, Sally Throgmorton, the Misses Chew, &c., &c. And then there was an almost continuous influx of visitors, chiefly from Spotsylvania, Caroline, and Culpeper, and a stream of travellers to and from Kentucky by way of Culpeper, Winchester, and Red Stone in Monongalia.

These people seem to have had a gay time — dining parties of twenty-five to thirty from house to house; quilting parties, winding up with a dance; balls at Sanford's, Bell's, and Alcocke's hotels in the winter, varied with hare, fox, and wolf-hunting, especially

when Major Willis and Hay Taliaferro came up with
twenty hounds.   In the summer they had fish-fries
and barbecues at Dade's Mill, Waugh's Ford, Wood's
Spring, Leathers' Spring, and Herndon's Spring.
Col. Taylor seems never to have missed an election ;
he always records the names of the candidates for
office and the number of votes for each.   He brings
before us Mr. Madison as candidate for Congress,
Assembly and Convention, addressing the people in
defence of the Constitution, to which the ignorant
were opposed.   He is said to have spoken from the
steps of the old Lutheran Church, now in Madison,
with the people standing in the snow, and the cold so
intense that the orator's ears were frost-bitten.   He
records the votes for General Stevens of Culpeper
as Presidential Elector, for French Strother for
Senator, and for Tom Barbour and C. Porter for
Assembly.   He tells us about vestry meetings which
elected Tom Barbour and William Moore deputies to
the Convention; of Col. Oliver Towles, Wm. Wirt,
Robert Taylor, &c., pleading at the bar.   We see the
ladies shopping at Lee's, and Shepherd's, and Taylor's,
and Wilson's stores, and the men playing at the five
batteries.   Weddings too seem to have been more
common than now.   Under the date of January 1786
he says: Wm. Madison and the ladies have just
returned from the marriage of Mordecai Barbour and
Miss Strode.   27th March, 1787, large company at
J. Taylor's, at the marriage of Tom Barbour and
Mary Taylor, by Rev. Mr. Stevenson.   July 1st, at
the marriage of John Bell and Judy Burnley, and
then he varies the scene by saying: " Went to church
2d Dec., and Mr. Waddell told the people that he had
heard that it would be agreeable to them for him not

to attend here again till March, and he would not."
1788, 24th March, election for Convention:—James
Madison 202 votes, James Gordon 187, C. Porter 34.
Madison's election gave great satisfaction. May
14th, 1788, James Madison, Jr., at Goodlet's school
examining the boys. The next marriage, Nov. 10th,
1789, Archy Tutt to Caty Pendleton, of Culpeper;
Dec. 8th, John Stevens to Polly Williams of Culpeper;
1790, then comes the marriage of Thos. Macon and
Sally Madison, and on the 5th of Sept., R. Williamson and Caty Pendleton; Oct. 10th, John Harrison
and Sally Barbour; Dec. 11th, Henry Bell and Betsy
Alcocke. 1791, Ch. Porter died. April 27th, James
Blair and Nelly Shepherd. 29th July, John Bell, of
Culpeper, died. B. Wood married Miss Porter. May
3d, Henry Fitzhugh and Betsy Conway. Nov., Wm.
Dade and Mrs. Sarah Dade. Nov. 29th, Joshua Fry
married Kitty Walker. 1794, James Madison mar-
ried Mrs. Todd. July 19th, Erasmus Taylor died,
eighty-three years old. 29th, Col. Thomas Barbour's
wife died. 1795, May 18th, Mrs. Sarah Thomas died,
eighty-four years of age. James Barbour, Jr., married
Lucy Johnson. Dec., James Bell married Hannah
Gwatkin. 22d, James Taylor, Jr., married Fanny
C. Moore. Thos. Bell (Courthouse) married Sally
Burnley. Jno. Walker (son of James) married Lucy
Wood, of Madison. 1796, Feb. 5th, Fortunatus
Winslow married Polly Alcocke. D. Turner married
Miss E. Pendleton, of Caroline. March 2d, James
Coleman (Springs) and Thos. Bell died. 5th, Henry
Pendleton married Elizabeth Pendleton, of Culpeper.
22d, Col. Richard Barbour married Polly Moore.
23d, Thos. Scott, of Madison, died. 26th, Col. T.
Moore died. Mrs. Alcocke, formerly Mrs. Dr. Walker,

died. Nov. 16th, Adam Darby married Betsy Shepherd. Dec. 3d, Reuben Smith married Milly Glassell. 19th, Anthony Buck married Mary Shepherd. 1797, March 14th, Baldwin Taliaferro married Ann Spotswood, of New Post. 16th, Hay Taliaferro married Sukey Conway, and my son and daughter went to the wedding — the horses ran away and they did not get back. Nov. 19th, Ambrose Macon married Miss Thomas. Dec. 7th, Camp Porter married a daughter of Jno. Alcocke. Wm. Mallory married Mary Gibson. 1798, March 12th, Rev. Mr. O'Neil and Phil. Barbour (son of Thomas) came here this morning. Mr. O'Neil had been to Tom Barbour's to marry T. Newman and Lucy Barbour. 1799, Jan. 8th, large company at James Taylor's, at the marriage of Thomas Crutchfield, and Col. James Barbour came home with me. G. Terrill had petition to Assembly for bridge at Barnett's Ford.

The churches in St. Thomas Parish are St. Thomas, Orange Courthouse, Rev. Jno. S. Hansbrough, Rector, who reported in 1876 eighty-six communicants.

Christ Church, Gordonsville, Rev. F. G. Scott, Rector, communicants (1876) forty-six.

BROMFIELD PARISH.

Bromfield was cut off from St. Mark's by Act of Assembly in 1752. The dividing line has been marked in the body of this work. Its western boundary starts from John Spotswood's corner on Crooked Run (near Wayland's Mill) and runs north by east to the junction of White Oak Run with the Rappahannock River; thus including what is now

Madison and Rappahannock Counties, and a small section of Culpeper. Bromfield, after this date, had its ministers, vestries, and records, of which there is now scarcely a trace. In the absence of such registers, I can only reconstruct the history of this parish with the few materials gleaned from different and distinct sources. The very name has been recently and unconsciously changed into Bloomfield, in which form it appears on the Journals of Convention ever since 1833, except in 1839 when it was represented by Jno. F. Conway, who restored the right name. After this one effort to recover its historical name, it relapsed into Bloomfield, and has been so called ever since. Even Bishop Meade calls it "Old Bloomfield Parish." The word is Saxon, and means Broomfield. Perhaps this is the origin of what we call in Virginia a broom-straw or broom-sedge field. However applicable the term may have been to the lower part of the parish (the Piney Woods), *Bloomfield* is more descriptive of the Piedmont portion, which had not then been developed. Let us hope that the lost name may be restored for history's sake.

We know the names of at least two of the old vestrymen of Bromfield, Martin Nalle and Ambrose Powell, who in 1754 negotiated with the vestry of St. Mark's about running the dividing line between the old and the new parish. Henry Field and Philip Clayton had been ordered in 1752 to attend the surveyor in running these lines. The courses threw "Tennant's Church" and the church in the Fork of Devil's Run and the Hazel River into Bromfield Parish. Later in the century there was a church at F. T., so called from the initials of

Frank Thornton being cut on an oak tree near the spring, that being a corner in his survey. There was also a church not far from the present site of Washington, near where Frank Slaughter now lives.

The first minister of Bromfield probably was the Rev. Adam Menzies, who had been a respectable schoolmaster, for I find in the "Fulham MSS." that he was licensed for Virginia, and his name is set down in 1754–5 as minister of Bromfield. There was also a James Herdman (1775), some of whose books are now in my possession (Sherlock's, Secker's, and Atterbury's sermons), which were bought in Rappahannock as the remnant of an old English parson's library. The late Samuel Slaughter, who died about 1857, in his 90th year, said that he, in his boyhood, went to school to a Rev. Mr. Harrison, minister of Bromfield. Thomas, great-grandson of Burr Harrison, of Chippawamsic (who was baptized at Westminster in December, 1637, and was the first of the family in Virginia), was the father of the late Philip Harrison of Richmond, and of Mrs. Freeman, mother of Mrs. McCoy, of Culpeper. In 17 90 there was a minister named Iredell who offici-ated at the South Church, four miles below Madison C. H. He was followed by O'Neil, an athletic Irishman, who was one of those old-time school-masters who believed in what Hudibras calls "Apos-tolic blows and knocks" more than in the Apostolic succession. He was a disciple of Solomon and never "spoiled the child by sparing the rod." He sus-pended them upon a stout negro's back when he ad-ministered the flagellations. He taught school near the Pine Stake Church, in the family of Col. Taliaferro, and also in Madison. The late Judge Barbour and the Hon. Jere and Dr. Geo. Morton were among his pupils, and retained a lively recollection of his discipline. The memory of that mother in Israel, Mrs. Sarah Lewis, already referred to, went back to O'Neil's time. The Rev. J. Woodville made occasional excursions to these churches, when vacant, and the Lutheran minister, Mr. Carpenter, baptized and buried the Episcopalians when without a pastor.

The leading Episcopal families who adhered to the church of their fathers through evil as well as good report, were the Lewises, Burtons, Vawters, Caves, Gibbs, Strothers, Thorntons, Barbours, Conways, Gibsons, Pannills, Gaines, and Beales. The last name reminds me that Reuben Beale was a Lay Delegate to the first Convention in 1789 and 1793. After the revival of the church in the Rev. Mr. Lamon's time (1834-5), when there were large accessions to its communion, the ministers have been the Rev. A. H. Lamon, deceased, Wm. T. Leavell, John Cole, deceased, R. T. Brown of Maryland, Joseph Earnest, deceased, Rev. Dr. Shield of Louisville, Ky., Wm. H. Pendleton, deceased, J. G. Minnegerode of Culpeper, Rev. Mr. Wroth of Baltimore, with occasional services by other clergymen. There is a church at Madison C. H. which, in 1834, had forty communicants whose names are now before me, a church at Woodville, and one at Washington. These churches have been so depleted by emigration to the south and west, and by infrequent and intermittent services, that they are hardly able to stand alone, and are now (Dec. 1876) like sheep scattered on the mountains, without a shepherd.

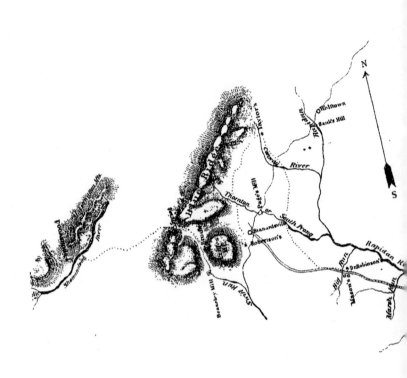

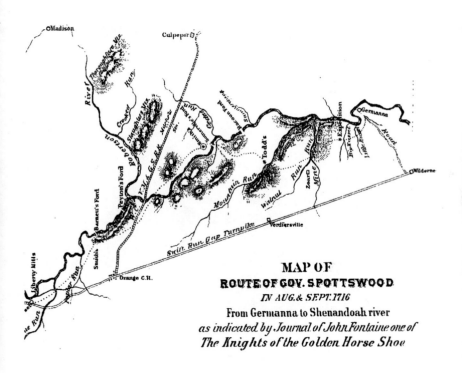

MAP OF
ROUTE OF GOV. SPOTTSWOOD
IN AUG.& SEPT. 1716
From Germanna to Shenandoah river
as indicated by Journal of John Fontaine one of
The Knights of the Golden Horse Shoe

Historical Excursions.

THE KNIGHTS OF THE GOLDEN HORSE-SHOE.

Sic juvat transcendere Montes.

Governor Spotswood's expedition over the great mountains, as he called it, is one of the most romantic passages in the history of Virginia. Indeed, it has been happily chosen as the theme of a romance by Dr. Caruthers, entitled "The Knights of the Horseshoe," a traditionary tale of the cocked hat gentry in the Old Dominion. The author seems to have used due diligence in gathering the fugitive traditions of this adventure which lingered dimly in the minds of his generation. The popular idea of this expedition seems to have been derived from the "traditionary tale," as the author fitly calls it. One is reluctant to unmask a popular idol by substituting facts for fancies and showing the historical basis upon which it stands. Until the publication of John Fontaine's journal, the facts known about this expedition were but few. Robert Beverly, one of the party, in his Preface to the History of Virginia, 1722, merely said, "I was with the present Governor at the head-spring of both these rivers (York and Rappahannock), and their fountains are in the highest ridge of mountains." The Rev. Hugh Jones, Chaplain to the House of Burgesses, in his Present State of Virginia (1724), says:—"Governor Spotswood when he undertook the great discovery

of a passage over the mountains, attended with a
sufficient guard of pioneers and gentlemen, with a
supply of provisions, passed these mountains and cut
his Majesty's name upon a rock upon the highest of
them, naming it Mt. George, and in complaisance to
him the gentlemen called the mountain next to it
Mt. Alexander.   For this expedition they were
obliged to provide a great quantity of horseshoes,
things seldom used in the eastern part of Virginia,
where there are no stones.   Upon which account the
Governor, upon his return, presented each of his
companions with a golden horseshoe, some of which
I have seen covered with valuable stones resembling
heads of nails, with the inscription on one side, ' Sic
juvat transcendere Montes.'   This he intended to
encourage gentlemen to venture backward and make
discoveries and settlements; any gentleman being
entitled to wear this golden shoe who could prove
that he had drunk his Majesty's health on Mt.
George."

It has always been assumed that Gov. Spotswood
communicated an account of his expedition to the
home government, and it tends to confirm this
assertion that Chalmers in his " Annals " says the
British Government penuriously refused to pay the
cost of golden horseshoes.   But nothing has yet
been produced from Spotswood on this subject.   The
present writer has recently gone through the Spotswood manuscripts recovered from England, whither
they had been carried by Feathershaugh, and which
are now the property of the Historical Society of
Virginia.   We only discovered one allusion to the
subject in these papers.   In a letter to the Board of
Trade, 1718, Spotswood says:—" The chief aim of

my expedition over the great mountains in 1716 was
to satisfy myself whether it was practicable to come
at the lakes. Having found an easy passage over
that great ridge of mountains hitherto deemed un-
passable, I discovered from the relations of Indians
which frequent these parts, that from the pass where
I was it was but three days' march to a great nation
of Indians, living on a river which discharges itself
into Lake Erie; and that from the west side of the
small mountain that I saw that lake is very visible.
The mountains on the other side of the great ridge
being smaller than those I passed, shows how easy a
matter it is to gain possession of these lakes." To
account for these crude notions of the geography of
the country it must be remembered that all west of
Germanna was at that time a vast unexplored
wilderness, covered by a dense forest, never trodden
by the foot of the white man, except the flying
rangers who hovered upon the frontiers of population to watch the Indians.

John Fontaine, son of Rev. James Fontaine
(Huguenot), and brother of the Rev. Peter Fontaine
and of the Rev. James Fontaine, clergymen of the
Church of England in Virginia, was an ensign in the
British army. He came to Virginia in 1713, for the
purpose of exploring the country and choosing lands
for the settlement of the family when they should
come over. He made the acquaintance of Governor
Spotswood at Williamsburg, and under his auspices
visited the new settlement at Germanna, and accompanied Spotswood to his Indian school at Christanna,
on the Meherrin River, and also on his expedition
over the great mountains. He kept a journal of his
daily doings, which furnishes the only authentic

H

account we have of this stirring adventure. His plain, unvarnished tale dispels the mist which the popular fancy had peopled with hostile Indians haunting the march, assassins stealing into camp at dead of night and committing murder, perpetrating massacres, and doing battle in the mountain passes. The recent publication of this journal rescues the facts from traditionary perversions and restores them to their true historical proportions. From him (an eye-witness) we learn that Governor Spotswood came from Williamsburg by way of Chelsea (King William) and Robert Beverly's (Middlesex), where the Governor left his chaise, and bringing Beverly along, came on horseback to Germanna, where, on the 26th August, 1716, they were met by other gentlemen, four Meherrin Indians, and two small companies of rangers. The names of the gentlemen of the party, deduced in part from the camps which were called after them, were: Governor Spotswood, John Fontaine, Robt. Beverly, the historian; Col. Robertson, Dr. Robinson, Taylor Todd, Mason, Captains Clonder, and Smith, and Brooke, the ancestor of the late Judge Brooke. Campbell says:—"The whole company was about fifty persons. They had a large number of riding and pack-horses, an abundant supply of provisions, and an extraordinary variety of liquors."

There have been divers opinions about the route which this gay company of young bloods pursued, and the gap at which they passed the mountains. The starting point (Germanna) is fixed, and the terminus, we think, by the light of Fontaine's Journal, is just as certain. We have seen that Beverly (of the party) says " he was with Governor Spotswood at the

head-springs of the York and Rappahannock Rivers."
We shall presently see that Fontaine says "we passed
from the head-waters of the Rappahannock to the
head-waters of the James in a few hours." Now as
Swift Run Gap is the only "pass" which the head-
waters of York, James, and Rappahannock rivers
approximate, and as Swift Run, a branch of the
James, flows down the eastern gorge of the gap from
a spring whose present site, description, and relations
to another spring flowing down the western declivity
correspond with Fontaine's account of them, we are
shut up to the conclusion that Swift Run Gap is the
historical pass. As to the intermediate course
between these fixed points nothing is certainly
known, except the first stages, viz. Expedition (Big
Russell) Run, Mine Run, Mountain Run (the last two
still retaining the names given them by these cava-
liers), and Rappahannock River at or near Somerville's Ford. So far the route seems plain. Our
theory, as seen by the map, is that, encountering
Clarke's Mountain at this point, they crossed the
river, which demonstrably then ran nearer the mountain than now, and proceeding up the flats until they
had flanked the mountain, recrossed to the highlands,
and passing through Jones', Holladay's, Bresee's, &c.,
encamped beyond Barnett's Ford, at a point where
they had a fine view of the Appalachian Mountains,
as they called them. Persons may well differ as to
the precise line of travel, and maintain their theories
by plausible arguments. All the points cannot now
be settled with absolute certainty, and are not material; the main point being the general course of
travel between Germanna and Swift Run Gap. The
theory of the map is that they continued their

journey on the south side of the Rapidan through
the beautiful bottoms of the forks of Poplar, Blue
and Marsh Runs, striking and crossing the river
again where it is very small.   That they returned
this way is confirmed by the fact that when they
reached a certain point on the Rapidan, Mr. Beverly
was so pleased with the land that he said he would
take out a patent for it.   Mr. B. Johnson Barbour's
title to his beautiful river-farm goes back to Beverly's
patent.   The accompanying map was kindly and
gratuitously constructed for us by Capt. Joseph J.
Halsey, a lawyer, versed in the lore of old land
patents and surveys, and a competent topographer,
after a patient study of all the materials we could
gather.   The map is based upon sketches of the
country about Germanna made by Rev. J. C. Willis,
of Indiantown, from his own surveys, and an outline
map of Mr. Brooking of the upper part of the route,
and upon Capt. Halsey's own surveys, supplemented
by his knowledge of the country, and aided by the
suggestions of Mr. Stevens of Stannardsville, and
other persons of the vicinage.   Messrs. Halsey,
Willis, and Brooking are all practical surveyors, and
represent the beginning, middle and end of the route.

But we must not detain the reader longer from
Fontaine's Journal, from which he can deduce his
own conclusions.   Those who have never read it will
find it a lively picture of the first company of gentlemen whose trumpet first waked the echoes of our
hills, and lifted the blue veil which hid from the eyes
of the white man the fair face of nature in the Valley
of Virginia.

JOURNAL OF MR. FONTAINE.

August 27th.—Got our tents in order and our horses shod.

29th.—In the morning we got all things in readiness, and about one we left the German-town, to set out on our intended journey. At five in the afternoon the Governor gave orders to encamp near a small river three miles from Germanna, which we call Expedition Run, and here we lay all night. The first encampment was called Beverly Camp, in honor of one of the gentlemen of our party. We made great fires, and supped, and drank good punch. By ten of the clock I had taken all of my ounce of Jesuit's bark, but my head was much out of order.

30th.—In the morning about seven of the clock the trumpet sounded to awake all the company, and we got up. One Austin Smith, one of the gentlemen with us, having a fever, returned home. We had lain upon the ground under cover of our tents, and we found by the pains in our bones that we had not had good beds to lie upon. At nine in the morning we sent our servants and baggage forward, and we remained because two of the Governor's horses had strayed. At half-past two we got the horses, at three we mounted, and at half an hour after four we came up with our baggage at a small river three miles on the way, which we call Mine River, because there was an appearance of a silver mine by it. We made about three miles more, and came to another small river, which is at the foot of a small mountain, so we encamped here and called it Mountain Run, and our camp we called Todd's Camp. We had good pasturage for our horses, and venison in abundance for ourselves, which we roasted before the fire on wooden forks, and so we went to bed in our tents. We made six miles this day.

31st.—At eight in the morning we set out from Mountain Run, and after going five miles we came upon the upper part of Rappahannock River. One of the gentlemen and I, we kept out on one side of the company about a mile, to have the better hunting. I saw a deer and shot him from my horse, but the horse threw me a terrible fall and ran away, we ran after him, and with a great deal of difficulty got him again ; but we could not find the deer I had shot, and we lost ourselves, and it was two hours before we could come upon the track of our company. About five miles farther we crossed the same river again, and two miles farther we met with a large bear, which one of our company shot and I got the skin. We killed several deer, and about two miles from the place where we killed the bear we encamped, upon the Rappahannock River. From our encampment we could see the Appalachian Hills very plain. We made large fires, pitched our tents, and cut boughs to lie upon, had good liquor, and at ten we went to sleep. We always kept a sentry at the Governor's door. We called this Smith's Camp. Made this day fourteen miles.

1st September.—At eight we mounted our horses and made the first five miles of our way through a very pleasant plain, which lies where Rappahannock River forks. I saw there the largest timber, the finest and deepest mould, and the best grass that I ever did see. We had some of our baggage put out of order and our company dismounted by hornets stinging the horses. This was some hindrance and did a little damage, but afforded a great deal of diversion. We killed three bears this day, which exercised the horses as well as the men. We saw two foxes, but did not pursue them; we killed several deer. About five of the clock we came to a run of water at the foot of a hill where we pitched our tents. We called the encampment Dr. Robinson's Camp, and the river Blind Run. We had good pasturage for our horses, and every one was cook for himself. We made our beds with bushes as before. This day we made thirteen miles.

2d.—At nine we were all on horseback, and after riding about five miles we crossed the Rappahannock River almost at the head, where it is very small. We had a rugged way; we passed over a great many small runs of water, some of which were very deep and others very miry. Several of our company were dismounted, some were down with their horses, and some thrown off. We saw a bear running down a tree, but it being Sunday we did not endeavor to kill anything. We encamped at five by a small river we called White Oak River, and called our camp Taylor's Camp.

3d.—About eight we were on horseback, and about ten we came to a thicket so tightly laced together that we had a great deal of trouble to get through. Our baggage was injured, our clothes torn all to rags, and the saddles and holsters also torn. About five of the clock we encamped almost at the head of James River, just below the great mountains. We called this camp Col. Robertson's camp. We made all this day but eight miles.

4th.—We had two of our men sick with the measles and one of our horses poisoned with a rattle-

snake. We took the heaviest of our baggage, our
tired horses, and the sick men, and made as convenient a lodge for them as we could, and left people
to guard them and to hunt for them. We had
finished this work by twelve, and so we set out.
The sides of the mountains were so full of vines and
briers that we were forced to clear most of the way
before us. We crossed one of the small mountains
on this side the Appalachian, and from the top of it
we had a fine view of the plains below. We were
obliged to walk up the most of the way, there being
abundance of loose stones on the side of the hill. I
killed a large rattlesnake here, and the other people
killed three more. We made about four miles, and
so came to the side of James River where a man
may jump over it, and there we pitched our tents.
As the people were lighting the fire there came out
of a large log of wood a prodigious snake, which they
killed, so this camp was called Rattlesnake Camp,
but otherwise it was called Brooke's Camp.

5th.—A fair day. At five we were mounted. We
were obliged to have axemen to clear the way in
some places. We followed the windings of James
River, observing that it came from the very top of
the mountains. We killed two rattlesnakes during
our ascent. In some places it was very steep, in
others it was so that we could ride up. About one
of the clock we got to the top of the mountain;
about four miles and a half and we came to the very
head-spring of James River, where it runs no bigger
than a man's arm from under a big stone. We drank
King George's health and all the royal family's at
the very top of the Appalachian mountains. About
a musket-shot from the spring there is another,

which rises and runs down to the other side. It goes westward, and we thought we could go down that way, but we met with such prodigious precipices that we were obliged to return to the top again. We found some trees which had been formerly marked, I suppose by the Northern Indians, and following these trees we found a good, safe descent. Several of the company were for returning, but the Governor persuaded them to continue on. About five we were down on the other side, and continued our way until about seven miles further, when we came to a large river, by the side of which we encamped. We made this day fourteen miles. I, being somewhat more curious than the rest, went on a high rock on the top of the mountain to see fine prospects, and I lost my gun. We saw when we were over the mountain the footing of elk and buffaloes and their beds. We saw a vine which bore a sort of wild cucumber, and a shrub with a fruit like unto a currant. We ate very good wild grapes. We called this place Spotswood's Camp, after our Governor.

6th.—We crossed the river, which we called Euphrates. It is very deep; the main course of the water is north; it is fourscore yards wide in the narrowest part. We drank some healths on the other side and returned, after which I went a-swimming in it. We could not find any fordable place except the one by which we crossed, and it was deep in several places. I got some grasshoppers and fished, and another and I we catched a dish of fish, some perch and a kind of fish they called chub. The others went a-hunting, and killed deer and turkeys. The Governor had graving irons, but could not grave anything, the stone was so hard. I graved my name on a tree by the river side, and the Governor buried a bottle with a paper enclosed, on which he writ that he took possession of this place in the name and for King George First of England. We had a good dinner, and after it we got the men together and loaded all their arms, and we drank the King's health in champagne and fired a volley, the Princess's health in Burgundy and fired a volley, and all the rest of the royal family in claret and a volley. We drank the Governor's health and fired another volley. We had several sorts of liquors, viz., Virginia red wine and white wine, Irish usquebaugh, brandy, shrub, two sorts of rum, champagne, canary, cherry punch, water, cider, &c. I sent two of the rangers to look for my gun which I dropped in the mountain; they found it and brought it to me at night, and I gave them a pistol for their trouble. We called the highest mountain Mount George, and the one we crossed over Mount Spotswood.

7th.—At seven in the morning we mounted our horses and parted with the rangers, who were to go farther on, and we returned homewards. We repassed the mountains, and at five in the afternoon we came to Hospital Camp, where we left our sick men and heavy baggage, and we found all things well and safe. We encamped here and called it Captain Clonder's Camp.

8th.—At nine we were all on horseback. We saw several bears and deer, and killed some wild turkeys. We encamped at the side of a run and called the place Mason's Camp. We had good forage for our horses, and we lay as usual. Made twenty miles this day.

9th.—We set out at nine of the clock, and before twelve we saw several bears, and killed three. One of them attacked one of our men that was riding after him and narrowly missed him; he tore his things that he had behind him from off the horse, and would have destroyed him had he not had immediate help from the other men and our dogs. Some of the dogs suffered severely in this engagement. At two we crossed one of the branches of the Rappahannock River, and at five we encamped on the side of the Rapid Ann, on a tract of land that Mr. Beverly hath design to take up. We made this day twenty-three miles, and called this Captain Smith's Camp. We ate part of one of the bears, which tasted very well, and would be good and might pass for veal if one did not know what it was. We were very merry, and diverted ourselves with our adventures.

10th.—At eight we were on horseback, and about ten, as we were going up a small hill, Mr. Beverly and his horse fell down, and they both rolled to the bottom; but there were no bones broken on either side. At twelve as we were crossing a run of water, Mr. Clonder fell in, so we called this place Clonder's Run. At one we arrived at a large spring, where we dined and drank a bowl of punch. We called this Fontaine's Spring. About two we got on horseback, and at four we reached Germanna.

Spotswood instituted what he called the Tramontane Order, in commemoration of the expedition, each gentleman being entitled to wear the golden horseshoe who could prove that he had drunk his Majesty's health on Mt. George. The golden horse-

shoes descended as heirlooms in several families.
Judge Brooke, in his autobiography, speaks of one
in the possession of Edmund Brooke, whose ancestor
was of the party. This gentleman died in Georgetown, D. C., and we had hoped to find the relic in his
daughter's possession, but it had been lost. Campbell speaks of the late Mrs. Bott, of Petersburg, a
descendant of Spotswood, having seen the miniature
horseshoe belonging to Spotswood, and that it was
small enough to be worn on a watch-chain. Spotswood probably had more than one of them, as we
find it said in the Byrd manuscripts that when
Spotswood made a treaty with the five nations of
Indians at Albany, in 1722, in which they bound
themselves not to pass the Potomac or the Blue
Ridge, the Governor told the Indians that they must
take particular notice of their speaker, and gave him
a golden horseshoe which he wore at his breast, and
bade the interpreter tell him that there was an inscription on it which signified that it would help him
to pass the mountains, and that when any of their
people should come to Virginia they must bring
that with them. These things are like dreams to
us now. With a population which has not only
transcended the Blue Ridge, but the Alleghany and
the Rocky Mountains, and reached the Golden Gate
of California, it is hard to realize that only 160 years
ago Germanna was a frontier post, and the great
West an unknown world, except to the wild Indian,
whose tribes have melted away before the pale faces
like snow before the sun, and whose barque, like that
of the crew of the fabled phantom ship, "rides on
and on, and anchored ne'er shall be."

GERMANNA.

Salve Posteritas!
Posteritas Germano-politana.

The German people is a political element in American civilization. The number of Germantowns in the United States is curious and suggestive. The oldest of these is the one in Pennsylvania, which was the scene of the battle of Germantown in the old Revolution, in which so many of the men of St. Mark's figured. It was established in 1683, under the auspices of Pastorius, to provide, as he said, a "pellace" or refuge from the judgments impending over the old world, and to Christianize the naked-going savages. He composed a noble Latin ode on the occasion, beginning—

Salve Posteritas!
Posteritas Germano-politana,

which Whittier has put beautifully into English verse, thus:

Hail to Posterity!
Hail, future men of Germanopolis!
Let the young generation, yet to be,
    Look kindly upon this;
Think how our fathers left their native land—
Dear German land! O sacred hearts and homes!—
        And where the wild beast roams,
        In patience planned
New forest homes, beyond the mighty sea,
        There undisturbed and free,
        To live as brothers of one family.
        What pains and cares befel,
        What trials and what fears,
Remember, and whenever we have done well,
        Follow our footsteps, men of coming years.

I

Where we have failed to do
Aught, or wisely live,
Be warned by us, the better way pursue,   ·
And knowing we were human, even as you,
Pity us and forgive.
Farewell, Posterity!
Farewell, dear Germany!
Forevermore farewell!

See Memorial Thomas Potts, Jr., by Mrs. James.)

Our Germanna was settled under the auspices of
Governor Spotswood in 1714, on a peninsula of 400
acres of land on the banks of the Rapidan.   These
Germans came directly from Oldensburg, or were a
remnant of a settlement planted under the auspices of
the Baron de Graffenreid in North Carolina, many
of whom were massacred by the Tuscarora Indians,
as related by Governor Spotswood in a letter of
October 1711, which is published in Perry's Collec-
tions from the archives of Fulham and Lambeth.
Spotswood says he had demanded the release of De
Graffenreid, the Chief of the Palatines and Swiss,
who had been taken prisoner, and was, he feared,
reserved for torture by fire. That these Germans
might have been the survivors of the massacre in
North Carolina is a mere conjecture, suggested by
the fact that De Graffenreid was the leader of both
parties.   I have just found in the Spotswood MSS.
the following paragraph in a letter of Governor
Spotswood to the Commissioners of Trade in England, dated May 1714:—"I continue to settle our
tributary Indians, and in order to supply that part
which was to have been covered by the Tuscarora
Indians, I have placed there a number of Protestant
Germans, built them a fort, furnished it with two
pieces of cannon and some ammunition, which will

awe the straggling parties of Northern Indians and
be a good barrier to all that part of the country.
These Germans were invited over some years ago by
the Baron De Graffenreid, who had her Majesty's
letter to the Governor to furnish them with land after
their arrival. They are generally such as have been
employed in their own country in mines, and say
they are satisfied there are divers kinds of minerals
where they are settled, and even a good appearance
of silver; but it is impossible to know whether those
mines will turn to account without digging some
depth — a liberty I shall not give them until I hear
from your Lordships."

These Germans landed at Tappahannock, and a
dispute arose between them and the captain of the
ship in which they sailed, about the money for their
passage. The captain refused to deliver their effects
until his demand was satisfied. Governor Spotswood
being present, proposed that if the Germans would
settle on his land and remain long enough to instruct
some of his young men in mechanical trades, he
would pay the bill. They consented, and hence the
settlement at Germanna. In 1714, John Fontaine
and John Clayton of Williamsburg visited Germanna,
and described it as follows:—"We went to the
German minister's house (they say), and finding
nothing to eat, lived upon our own provisions and
lay upon straw. Our beds not being easy, we got up
at break of day, and in a hard rain walked about the
town, which is palisaded with stakes stuck in the
ground close to each other, and of substance to resist
musket-shot. There are but nine families, and nine
houses all in a line; and before every house, twenty
feet distant, they have sheds for their hogs and their

hens; so that hog-stys on one side and dwellings on
the other make a street. The place paled in is a
pentagon, regularly laid out; and in the centre is a
block-house with five sides, answering to the five sides
of the great enclosure. There are loop-holes in it,
from which you may see all the inside of the enclosure. This is intended for a retreat in case of their
not being able to defend the palisades from the
Indians. They use the block-house for Divine service. They go to prayers once a day and have two
services Sunday. We went to hear them perform
their service, which is done in their own language,
which we did not understand, but they seem very
devout and sing the psalms very well. This settlement is (1714) thirty miles from any inhabitant.
They live very miserably. For want of provisions
we were obliged to go. We got from the minister a
bit of smoked beef and cabbage, and gave him thirty
shillings and took our leave. In less than three
hours on our way we saw nineteen deer; and we
lodged at Mr. Smith's, at the Falls of the Rappahannock."

We must now let the Germans speak for themselves.
In the archives of the English society for propagating the Gospel in foreign parts is the following
memorial:—"The case of thirty-two Protestant
German families settled in Virginia humbly sheweth,
that twelve Protestant German families, consisting
of about fifty persons, arrived April 1714, in Virginia,
and were there settled near Rappahannock River.
That in 1717, twenty Protestant German families,
consisting of about four-score persons, came and
settled down near their countrymen. And many
more Germans and Swiss are likely to come. For

the ministries of religion there will be a necessity for a small church and for a minister, who shall catechise and perform Divine offices among them in the German tongue, which is the only language they do yet understand. That there came indeed over with the first twelve German families a minister, named Henry Haeger — a very sober, honest man, about seventy-five years old; but he being likely soon to be past service, we have empowered Mr. J. C. Zollicoffer, of St. Gall, Switzerland, to go to Europe and obtain subscriptions from pious Christians towards building a church, and bringing over with him a young German minister to assist Mr. Haeger, and to succeed him when he shall die; to get him ordained in England by the Right Rev. Bishop of London, and to bring over with him the Liturgy of the Church of England, translated into High Dutch, which they are desirous to use in public worship. But this settlement consisting of only mean (poor) persons, utterly unable to build a church and support an assistant minister, they humbly implore the countenance, &c., of the Bishop of London and other Bishops, and the venerable society for propagating the Gospel in foreign parts, that they would take the case under their pious consideration and grant their usual allowance for the support of a minister, and if it may be so, subscribe something towards the building of their church, and they shall ever pray that the Lord may reward their beneficence here and hereafter." The above petition was sent in 1719.

In the year 1720 Spotsylvania was cut off from Essex, and the Parish of St. George, coterminous with the county, was erected in 1721. Governor Spotswood fixed the seat of justice at Germanna, and the first court, composed of John Taliaferro and others, was holden 1st August, 1722. An appropriation was made by the General Assembly of £500 for a church, a prison, a pillory and stocks. The Act of Assembly contains this clause, doubtless for the benefit of the Germans: "Because foreign Protestants may not understand English readily, if any such shall entertain a minister of their own, they and their tithables shall be free from taxes for ten years."

By the help of Governor Spotswood a church was built, and Spotsylvania County, named after Spotswood, and St. George's Parish began their career at Germanna, named from the Germans and Queen Anne. Governor Spotswood soon after made his home at Germanna. The Rev. Hugh Jones, in his "Present State of Virginia," published about 1724, thus describes Germanna:—"Beyond Governor Spotswood's furnace, within view of the vast mountains, he has founded a town called Germanna, from the Germans sent over by Queen Anne, who are now removed up further. Here Spotswood has servants and workmen of most handicraft trades; and he is building a church, courthouse, and dwelling-house for himself, and has cleared plantations about it, encouraging people to come and settle in that uninhabited part of the country, lately erected into a county. Beyond this (continues Jones) is seated the colony of the Germans Palatine."

These Germans Palatine were probably the founders of Germantown in Fauquier. However this may be, it is certain that the records of Fauquier develop the fact that in 1718 Jacob Spillman, John Hoffman, John and Herman Fishback, Peter Hitt, Jacob

Holtzclaw, and William Weaver, not finding room at Germanna, moved to Germantown. Only three of these (Hoffman, Fishback and Weaver) having been naturalized, they were sent to enter lands at Germantown. The title was in these three, and they were to make leases for ninety-nine years. The patent was issued in 1724. Copies of the leases are on record. Tillman Weaver, in his last will (1754, Dec. 14th), devises property to Tillman W., to Ann, wife of Jno. Kemper, and Mary, wife of Herman Hitt, Eva, wife of Samuel Porter, Jacob, Elizabeth, Catharine, &c. Peter Hitt in his will, 1771, devises to John, Jos., Herman, Peter, and to Mary, wife of Jacob Rector. Peter Hitt married Sarah James, and Jos. Hitt married Mary Coons. Several of these persons have their representatives in Fauquier, Culpeper and Madison Counties.

Colonel Byrd, already quoted, said that in 1732, while on a visit to Colonel Spotswood, he saw the ruinous tenements which they, the Germans, had occupied at Germanna, and adds that they had moved higher up to the forks of the Rappahannock (the Rapidan) to lands of their own, which must mean what is now the County of Madison, which lies within that fork. From the testimony of these witnesses the Germans must have migrated to Madison before 1724. The tradition is that they were disgusted with the poverty of the soil and the harsh treatment of their overseers in the mines, and resolved to seek their fortunes on the banks of the Robinson River; and from them has descended the very thrifty German element in the population of Madison County. What was the fate of their petition to London for a minister is not known. Had it suc-

ceeded we might have had a flourishing German
Episcopal church in Virginia. The Church of England being subject to the State, and the British
Ministry being generally governed in their policy to
the Church by considerations of political expediency,
may not have acted in the premises. However that
may have been, the tradition is that our German
friends procured subscriptions in Europe for building
a Lutheran church, which was erected about 1740,
near the junction of White Oak Run and the Robinson
River, and still stands in good condition. It is in
the form of a Maltese cross. Money was also raised
in Europe to buy a pipe-organ of good size, which I
believe is still in use. Subscriptions were taken in
Sweden too, perhaps for a communion service and
other purposes, and the King of Sweden was said to
have been one of the subscribers. General Banks of
Madison, we are told, had seen one of these subscrip-
tion papers. The church was endowed, held a glebe,
and has money at interest. By the kindness of
Governor Kemper I have a copy of the deed from
William Carpenter to Michael Cook and Michael
Smith, wardens and trustees of the German church,
and people inhabiting the fork of Rappahannock
River, in St. Mark's Parish and County of Spotsylvania, and their successors, for a glebe for the use of
the minister of the said German people and his
successors, a tract of land in the first fork of the
Rapidan River, containing one hundred and ninety-
three acres, more or less, &c. The deed is dated
1733, and signed, sealed and delivered by William
Carpenter in the presence of Jno. Waller, Robert
Turner, Ed. Broughton, James King and William
Henderson. This Michael Cook was no doubt the

same who, with George Woots, was appointed by the vestry in 1729 to count all the tobacco-plants from the mouth of the Robinson River up to the Great Mountains, including Mark Jones's plantation. The services in this church were originally in German, then once a month in English, and subsequently entirely in the English tongue.

Our interest in the history of this church is enhanced by the interchange of courtesies between the Lutherans and Episcopalians. The late Samuel Slaughter of this county remembered to have seen these Lutherans, when they had no minister of their own, come to Buck Run Episcopal church in Culpeper to receive the holy communion; and the late venerable Mrs. Sarah Lewis, the great-grandmother of Mrs. Dr. Robert Lewis of Culpeper, remembered when the Lutheran minister, Mr. Carpenter, used to baptize and perform other ministerial offices for the Episcopalians of Madison when they had no minister. Many of the first grist-mills on the Robinson River and its tributaries were built by German mechanics. The first German settlers are said to have suffered occasionally from the incursions of the Indians. There is a tradition that the last person killed by the Indians in this region was murdered near what is now New Hope Church. There are some large Old German Bibles extant which have descended as heirlooms from the primitive Germans. We are indebted to the venerable John Spotswood of Orange Grove, and to Dr. Andrew Grinnan of Madison, for some of the traditions referred to in the above chapter.

EXTRACT FROM THE DIARY OF CAPTAIN PHILIP SLAUGHTER,

BEGINNING IN 1775 AND CONTINUED TO 1849.

December 4th, 1849.—I am this day 81 years old. I was born in 1758 at my grandfather's, Major Philip Clayton's, who lived at Catalpa, where the Hon. J. S. Barbour now lives. My father, Col. James Slaughter, then lived on the Rappahannock River where Jones Green now lives. I went to school to John Wigginton, a first-rate English teacher in the Little Fork. My father sold this farm to Gavin Lawson, and bought another of his brother, Col. Francis Slaughter, near Culpeper C. H., where Samuel Rixey now lives. When we moved to the latter place, I went to write in the clerk's office with my grandfather, Major Clayton, who did the duties of that office for Roger Dixon, the clerk, whose home was in the lower country. After Dixon's death, John Jameson, who had served a regular apprenticeship in the clerk's office, was made clerk of the county. After several years' service in the office with Clayton and Jameson, my father withdrew me and sent me to a "Grammar School" of which Adam Goodlet (a Scotchman) was master, and which was the first public school in which Latin and Greek were taught in Culpeper County.*

After going to school to Goodlet 18 months, the American Revolution began, and I, not yet 17 years old, entered in Capt. John Jameson's company

---

* Adam Goodlet afterwards taught school in the Taylor Settlement in Orange. Col. F. Taylor often speaks of him in his diary, and mentions James Madison, Jr., (the future President) examining Goodlet's scholars.

of minute-men. Culpeper, Fauquier, and Orange
having agreed to raise a regiment, with Lawrence
Taliaferro of Orange as Colonel, Edward Stevens of
Culpeper as Lieutenant-Colonel, and Thomas Marshall of Fauquier as Major, the regiment met in
Major Clayton's old field, near Culpeper C. H., to
drill, in strong brown linen hunting-shirts, dyed
with leaves, and the words "Liberty or Death"
worked in large white letters on the breast, buck-
tails in each hat, and a leather belt about the
shoulders with tomahawk and scalping-knife. In a
few days an express came from Patrick Henry, commander of the First Virginia Continental Regiment,
saying that Dunmore had attempted to carry the
military stores from the magazine at Williamsburg
to the ships, &c. We marched immediately, and in
a few days were in Williamsburg. The people hearing that we came from the backwoods, and seeing
our savage-looking equipments, seemed as much
afraid of us as if we had been Indians. We took
pride in demeaning ourselves as patriots and gentlemen, and the people soon treated us with respect
and great kindness. Most of us had only fowling-
pieces and squirrel-guns. Dunmore having gone on
board of a British man-of-war, half of the minute-
men were discharged.

My father, Col. James Slaughter, with Col. Marshall and others, had the honor of being in the first
battle (the Great Bridge) fought in Virginia. I was
sent home to school. In the spring of 1776 I again
left school and entered in Col. John Jameson's
troop of cavalry for three years. But before we
marched I was appointed by the Committee of
Safety of Culpeper a Lieutenant in Capt. Gabriel

Long's company of riflemen, and we marched to join the army under Washington in New York. In 1777 we were attached to the 11th Continental Regiment, commanded by Daniel Morgan.

Lt. Slaughter was promoted to a captaincy in 1778, and served during the war, being in the battles of Brandywine, Germantown, &c. He was one of the sufferers at Valley Forge. His messmates were the two Porterfields, Johnson, and Lt. John (Chief Justice) Marshall. They were reduced sometimes to a single shirt, having to wrap themselves in a blanket when that was washed; not one soldier in five had a blanket. The snow was knee-deep all the winter, and stained with the blood from the naked feet of the soldiers. From the body of their shirts the officers had collars and wrist-bands made to appear on parade.

Capt. Slaughter kept a diary of his campaigns, which was lost in the wreck of so many fine libraries in the late war. Among the many anecdotes with which it abounded was the following concerning the late Chief Justice Marshall, at a camp on a night or two before the battle of Brandywine:—"At ten in the night we were aroused from sleep. Lt. Marshall had raked up some leaves to sleep on; he had pulled off one of his stockings in the night (the only pair of silk stockings in the regiment), and not being able to find it in the dark, he set fire to the leaves, and before we saw it a large hole had been burnt in it. He pulled it on so, and away we went," &c.

Capt. Slaughter's diary after the Revolution is preserved to 1849, when he died and was buried in Richmond.

LEWIS LITTLEPAGE.

As was said in the text of this history, the Rev. J. Stevenson married Fanny, the sister of Lewis Littlepage. This gentleman was born in Hanover County, Va., on 19th December, 1762, and died in Fredericksburg, July 19th, 1802. His career was brief, brilliant and unique ; and yet there are but few who seem to have heard of the battles, sieges, fortunes he had passed, the many accidents by flood and field, and his hair-breadth 'scapes, &c. His name has nearly lapsed from history, or rather he never had a niche in our temple of fame ; for Europe, and not America, was the theatre on which he played his part. I am indebted to Dr. Payne, the great-grandson of Mr. Stevenson, for an original letter, in which he narrates to his family the story of his life from 1785 to 1798. From the Memoirs of Elkanah Watson I am able to supply some incidents of his life up to the time when the narrative in his own letter begins.

Mr. Watson says:—" During my residence at Nantes I became intimately acquainted with Lewis Littlepage, one of the most remarkable characters of the age. He arrived in Nantes during the winter of 1779–80 on his way to Madrid, under the patronage of Mr. Jay, our stern and able minister to the court of Spain. He was then a mere youth, of fine manly figure, with a dark, penetrating black eye, and a physiognomy peculiar and striking. At that early period he was regarded as a prodigy of genius and acquirements. When I again heard of him he had separated from Mr. Jay's family, and entered as a volunteer aide to the Duke de Cuillon at the siege of

K

Minorca. At the attack of Gibraltar he was on one of the floating batteries, and was blown up, but saved. He participated in a conspicuous manner in the thrilling incidents of that memorable siege. After his catastrophe in the floating battery he got a situation on the Spanish admiral's ship, and in one of the engagements he stood upon the quarter-deck during the battle and sketched the various pontoons of the fleet. On the return of the Spanish fleet to Cadiz he was sent with an officer to Madrid with dispatches, and exhibited to the minister a curious and scientific view of the battle, and was received with great applause and distinction at the court of Madrid. In the April following the close of the war I dined with him at Dr. Franklin's, in Passy, and saw the sketch. At Paris and Versailles he moved in the first circles and attracted marked attention. In June he made a visit to my bachelor hall in Berkeley Square, London. I never saw him again. He made the tour of Europe and established himself at Warsaw, and became, in effect, Prime Minister, went to St. Petersburg as ambassador from Poland, acquitted himself with distinguished ability, and became one of the favorites of the Empress Catherine," &c.

The following letter of Lewis Littlepage to Lewis Holliday takes up the story of his life where Watson's narrative ends, and completes the account of his eventful career in Europe.

ALTONA, *9th January*, 1801.

DEAR SIR :—

I have this day received your letter of the 22nd August, 1800 . . . Since my existence is called in question, I give you, for the satisfaction of my family and friends, a short account

of all that has happened to me in Europe since 1785. On the
2nd March, 1786, I was sworn into the King of Poland's
Cabinet as his first confidential secretary, with the rank of
Chamberlain. In February, 1787, I was sent to negotiate a
treaty with the Empress of Russia at Kiovia, which I effected.
The same year I was sent as secret and special envoy to the
court of France to assist in the negotiations for the grand
Quadruple Alliance, which failed. In 1788 I was recalled, and
sent to Prince Potemkin's army in the Turkish war, where I
commanded a division, acting at the same time in a political
character. In 1789 I was compelled to leave Poland and travel
to Italy. Shortly after I received orders to repair to Madrid
upon a high political mission, in which I completely succeeded. In 1790 I was recalled from Spain and ordered to
wait ultimate instructions at Paris. I afterwards received
orders to repair by the way of Berlin to Warsaw for the
revolution of the 3d May, 1791. In 1792 120,000 Russians
invaded Poland. I was nominated Aide-de-camp-general to
the King, with the rank of Major-General. He signed the
confederation of Fargowitz, and in April, 1793, sent me once
more as his special envoy to Petersburg to prevent the
division of Poland. I was stopped by the Russian Government on the road, and the division took place. In 1794
Kosciusko and Madalinski began another revolution in
Poland. On 17th April the garrison and inhabitants of Warsaw rose in arms against the Russians; to save the life of my
unfortunate friend and king I was obliged to take part with
Poland, and that dreadful battle ended in the slaughter of
10,000 Russians. The Empress Catherine II. never for-
gave me my conduct upon that occasion. She was more
irritated against me by hearing that I had consented to accept
as commander-in-chief under the revolutionary government,
although I was destined to act against Russia. My having
assisted in repelling the Russian armies in their attempt to
storm Willna, gave also offence. In short, I had gone so far
in the revolution that I should have gone much farther had I
not been defeated with my friend Prince Joseph Poniatoski,
the King's nephew, by the late King of Russia on the 26th
August, 1794. That event lost me all my popularity. It was
very near getting me hanged, for I was regarded as the acting

person, although, upon my honor, Prince Poniatoski acted
that day against my advice. The King of Russia attacked us
with about three times our force, both in men and artillery,
and Kosciusko afforded us no support until we were beaten
beyond redemption, although neither his left nor centre were
engaged the whole day otherwise than in cannonading.

After the battle of 26th August I took no further part in
military affairs until the storming of Prague, which cost the
lives of 22,000 Polanders. On the 7th January, 1795, the King
of Poland was taken from Warsaw by the Russians to be con-
veyed to Grodno. I was separated from him by express
orders of the Empress, and it was hinted to me that nothing
less than my former services in the Turkish war could have
saved me from sharing the fate of the other chiefs of the revolution of 1794. After the departure of the King I set out for
Vienna, but was immediately ordered to leave that metropolis,
which produced a public altercation between me and the
Austrian ministry, but which ended to my satisfaction, as
Russia came forward and did me justice. The King of
Prussia, Frederick William II., afterwards allowed me to
return to Warsaw, then under his dominion, where I remained
until the death of the Empress Catherine II. I was then
invited to go to Petersburg with the King of Poland, but
refused unless reparation was made to me for the treatment I
had recently experienced. The Emperor said that "all that
regarded his mother; as he had given no offence, he should
make no reparation." I perhaps might have gone at last to
Russia, but was prevented by the sudden death of my friend,
my master, my more than father, Stanislaus Augustus, King
of Poland, who expired at Petersburg 12th Feb'y, 1798. After
that melancholy event a long correspondence took place
between the Emperor of Russia and myself, which ended in
his paying me in a very noble manner the sum assigned me by
the King of Poland as a reward of my long and dangerous
services.

I arrived in Hamburg in October last. My intention was to
go either to France or England, but I found myself strangely
embroiled with both these governments. I have settled
matters in France, but not yet in England. The ministers
there persist in believing me to be sent upon a secret envoy

from the Emperor of Russia, who is now at variance with England. God knows I am sick of European politics. I intended to have spent the winter in Hamburg, but was driven from that sink of iniquity by a most atrocious plot against my life and fortune. The latter is in safety, and should I perish even here under the hospitable government of Denmark, I shall leave nine or ten thousand pounds sterling so disposed of that my assassins cannot prevent its coming to my family. That sum is all I have saved from the wreck of my fortunes in Poland. In the spring I shall proceed to America, either by the way of France or directly from hence, provided I escape the daggers and poison with which I am threatened here.

My duty and affection to my mother, and kindest remembrance to all relations and friends.

Ever yours, my dear Sir,

LEWIS LITTLEPAGE.

LEWIS HOLLIDAY.

If the adventurous career of Lewis Littlepage needed confirmation, incidental proof and illustration of it will be found in the personal souvenirs devised by him to Waller Holladay and inherited by Col. Alexander Holladay, by whom they were kindly shown to the author :

1. The original patent conferring the position of chamberlain upon Lewis Littlepage upon his entrance into the Polish Cabinet, 1787, signed by the King.

2. The original patent of Knighthood of the Order of St. Stanislaus, 1790, signed by the King.

3. The letter from the Prince of Nassau requesting the Marshal de Ligno to give Lewis Littlepage a captaincy in the regiment Royale l'Allemande, reciting Littlepage's distinguished service at Port Mahon and Gibraltar.

4. The letter of the Duque de Cuillon assigning Lewis Littlepage to his staff.

5. The letter of Count Florda Blanca recommending Lewis Littlepage.

6. The passport of Lewis Littlepage for his mission to France.

7. Lewis Littlepage's gold-hilted rapier presented to him by the Queen of Spain.

8. Lewis Littlepage's gold key, his badge as chamberlain to the King of Poland.

9. The portrait of the King of Poland presented to Lewis Littlepage by the King on their final parting at Grodno.

Dr. Payne has too the insignia of Littlepage's knighthood, the Star of the Order of Stanislaus. In the centre is a convex silver plate, on which, formed of small ruby sets, are the initials S. A. R., Stanislaus Augustus Rex; surrounding this, wrought with gold thread, is the motto, *Incitat Proemiando.* Around this is a brilliant green border with gilt leaves. The rays of the star are silver spangles.

THE TOBACCO PLANT.

A very curious article might be written on the literature of tobacco, involving its relation to the church and the state, and its influence on the individual mind and body, on manners and habits, and the general wealth and happiness of the world. Such an article might be illustrated by the authority of statesmen, lawyers, medical men, merchants, farmers, and political economists, and adorned with gems of wisdom and of wit from nearly all the English scholars and poets, from King James's " Counterblast" to Charles Lamb's " Farewell to Tobacco,"

in which praises and curses alternate with amusing
felicity. It is interwoven with the history of Virginia at every stage of its progress. In colonial
times many Acts of Assembly were passed regulat-
ing its culture, and one office of the early vestries
was to appoint reputable freeholders to count tobacco
plants in each parish. Thus, as early as 1728, Goodrich Lightfoot and Robert Slaughter counted the
plants from the mouth of Mountain Run (in what
is now Culpeper) up to Joseph Howe's plantation,
and across to the mouth of the Robinson River;
Robert Green and Francis Kirtley on the other side
of Mountain Run to the North River; George Woots
and Michael Cook from the mouth of the Robinson
River up to the Great Mountains. The salaries of
ministers and civil officers were paid in tobacco, and
it, or notes representing it in the warehouses, were
the currency of the country. Some of these notes
are now before us. Parishes too were known as
"Orinoco" and "Sweet-scented" parishes, according
to the kind of tobacco grown in them. The salary
of a minister was 16,000 lbs. of tobacco, the value of
which varied from £40 to £80 in money. A sweet-
scented parish was worth much more than an
Orinoco parish. There was a deduction of 8 per
cent. for cash, and tobacco was sometimes as low as
six shillings current money. A minister's tobacco
was worth less than other like bulks of tobacco,
because it was so mixed. Many flourishing towns,
as Dumfries and Falmouth, &c., where Scotch merchants grew rich in this trade, sprang up in Virginia.
In Glasgow there is now a "Virginia Street," and
that city received a great impulse from becoming the
entrepot whence the farmers-general of France derived their supplies of tobacco from Virginia.

The Pine Tree and its Fruits—Salaries paid in Tar.

These two were subjects of legislation. Tar was
once in great demand for tarring the roofs of public
and private buildings. Special instructions were
given by the General Assembly of Virginia for pre-
paring pine-trees by stripping the bark from the
trunk of the trees, eight feet from the root, leaving a
small slip to keep the tree alive, when in a short
time, it was said, the sun would draw the turpentine
to the surface, and the whole trunk would become
light-wood.

It may not generally be known that towards the
North Carolina line, where little or no tobacco was
grown, the minister was paid in tar, pitch, and pork;
so says the Rev. Mr. Bagg in his report (1724) to the
Bishop of London.

Genealogies

Many of these family-trees had their roots in
Great Britain ages ago ; but it would take too much
space to trace them there. As a general rule,
we limit ourselves to the branches which were
transplanted in Virginia. If our notices of some of
these families are more extended than those of
others, it is because the former were better known
to us. Our design in printing these genealogies is
to gratify a natural desire, which most persons
feel, to know something of their forefathers, and to
show how family-trees in a few generations inter-
lock their branches. It is more creditable to
transmit an honorable name to one's children than
it is to derive it from one's ancestors, and to be
descended from good and true men than from a
long line of unworthy forefathers, even though it be
a line of kings and queens. But it seems to be un-
natural and irrational to attach more value to the
pedigrees of horses and herds than to the pedigrees
of men and women. One end of history is to reproduce the past for the gratification and instruction of
the present; and it is surely (at least) an innocent
curiosity to look back at those who in the past
century cleared the land which we now till, and who
laid the foundation of the institutions under which
we live.

Explanation of the abbreviations to be found in the genealogies:—*m.* means married; *ch.*, child or children; *dau.*, daughter, and *d. s. p.*, died without offspring.

THE BARBOUR FAMILY.

This family is of Scotch origin. There was a John Barbour who was Archdeacon of Old Aberdeen as early as 1357. He was the author of the historical poem on the Life and Actions of King Robert Bruce. Whether he was the root in Scotland of the branches of the family in Virginia, the writer does not know. Our relations are with James Barbour, the first of the name in what is now Culpeper. He was one of the first vestrymen of St. Mark's Parish at its organization at Germanna in 1731, and served in that office until the division of the parish in 1740, which threw him into the new parish of St. Thomas in Orange County, where he lived. If the old register of St. Thomas Parish had been preserved, we should doubtless have found his name as vestryman there. Among his children were 1st James, who represented Culpeper in the House of Burgesses in 1764. He was the father of Mordecai Barbour, who married a daughter of John Strode of Fleetwood in Culpeper, and of Thomas, Richard, and Gabriel, of whom the last three migrated to Kentucky. The Hon. John S. Barbour, M. C., brilliant at the bar and in the legislative halls, was the son of Mordecai and Miss Strode. He married Miss Beirne of Petersburg, and their children are, 1st. John S. Barbour, President of the Virginia Midland Railroad, who married a daughter of Henry Dangerfield of Alexandria ; 2d. James, member of Assembly and Convention, who married Miss Beckham ; 3d. Alfred, deceased ; 4th. Dr. Edwin Barbour ; 5th. Sally; 6th. Eliza (Mrs. George Thompson).

Thomas, son of James 1st, represented Orange in the Assembly in 1775, and St. Thomas Parish in the Convention in 1785-86-90. He married Isabella Thomas, daughter of Philip Pendleton. Their children were, 1st. Dr. Richard, and 2d. Thomas, who died in their youth ; 3d. Hon. Philip P. Barbour, Speaker of Congress, and of the Convention of 1829-30, and Justice of the Supreme Court U. S. He married Frances Todd, daughter of Benjamin Johnson of Orange. His children were : 1st. Philippa, who married Judge Field of Culpeper ; 2d. Elizabeth, who married John J. Ambler of Jacquelin Hall, Madison County ; 3d. Thomas, M. D., who married Catherine Strother of Rappahannock County, he died in St. Louis of cholera in 1849 ; 4th. Edmund Pendleton, who married Harriet, daughter of Col. John Stuart of King George, and died in 1851 ; 5th. Quintus, who married Mary, daughter of James Somerville of Culpeper ; 6th. Sextus, died in St. Louis ; 7th. Septimus, died in infancy. The Hon. P. P. Barbour died in Washington, attending the Supreme Court, February, 1841. His widow died April, 1872, aged 85.

4th James, son of Thomas and grandson of James 1st, was born June 10th, 1775. He was Governor of Virginia, Senator of U. S., Minister to England, Secretary of War, &c. Besides their other qualities, the two brothers had a wondrous faculty of speech in conversation and in the forum. James married, October 29th, 1792, Lucy, daughter of Benjamin John-

son. Their children were:—1st. Benjamin Johnson
Barbour, who died in 1820 in the 20th year of his age ;
2. James, who died November 7th, 1857 ; 3. Benjamin
Johnson Barbour, born June 14th, 1821, and married
November 17th, 1844, Caroline Homoesel, daughter
of the late eminent Dr. George Watson of Richmond.
Mr. Barbour inherits the genius of his father, informed by rare culture, but he follows the example
of his great-grandfather, and is content to be warden
of the church.   He was elected to Congress in 1865;
but the representatives of Virginia of that year
were not admitted to their seats.   4th. Lucy, daughter
of Governor Barbour, married (1822) John Seymour
Taliaferro, who was unhappily drowned in 1830 ; 5th.
Frances Cornelia Barbour married William Handy
Collins, a distinguished lawyer of Baltimore.

Among the daughters of Col. Thos. Barbour were:
1. Lucy, who married Thos. Newman and had three
daughters, Mrs. Macon, Mrs. Welch, and Wilhelmina,
and one son, James Barbour Newman.   2. Nelly,
married Martin Nalle of Culpeper, father of P. P.
Nalle, warden of St. Paul's Church, who married first
Miss Wallace, and second Miss Zimmerman, and is
the father of Mrs. Steptoe, wife of the Rector of St.
Paul's.   Cordelia Nalle married Joseph Hiden of
Orange, father of Rev. J. C. Hiden (Baptist), Greenville, S. C.   Edmonia Nalle married William Major,
Esq., of Culpeper; Fanny Nalle married John C.
Hansbrough (lawyer); Martinette Nalle married
Blucher Hansbrough of Culpeper; Lucetta Nalle
married George Booton of Madison; Jane Nalle
married George Clark of Washington, D. C.; Thos.
Nalle married Miss Hooe of Fredericksburg; Ben-
jamin Johnson Nalle died unmarried; and Sarah

Ellen Nalle married Col. Garrett Scott, father of Rev.
T. G. Scott of Christ Church, Gordonsville, Va.
Sally, daughter of Thomas Barbour, married Gabriel
Gray, and had daughters, Mrs. S. F. Leake, Mrs.
William Anderson, Mrs. R. W. Anderson, and Mrs.
Cowles. Mary, daughter of Thomas Barbour, married
Daniel Bryan — children, Mrs. Lathrop, Mrs. Judge
Wylie, Mrs. Brown, and two sons, B. Bryan and Wm.
Bryan.

James Barbour, the head of the foregoing family,
took out a patent for land on the Rapidan in 1734.

On the farm of Col. Garrett Scott in Orange is a
granite tombstone just as old as St. Mark's Parish.
The inscription is as follows: Here lyeth the body of
Jane, wife of John Scott, who was born ye 28th Dec.,
1699, and departed this life ye 28th April, 1731. This
farm is in direct lineal descent to the present owner
from a grant known as the "Todd Grant," from the
Crown of England.

THE CARTER FAMILY.

The first of this name in Virginia was Jno. Carter
of Corotoman, who died in 1669. A chart of his
descendants would fill this book. I limit this notice
to those known to the writer in St. Mark's Parish.
Robert, called King Carter, was the son of John 1st,
by his wife Sarah Ludlowe. Robert *m.* (1688) Judith
Armstead, and among their children was John, who
(1723) *m.* Eliza Hill of Shirley, and their third son
Edward of Blenheim *m.* Sarah Champe, and their
daughter Eliza *m.* William Stanard of Roxbury,
Spotsylvania, who was the grandfather of Virginia
Stanard, who *m.* Samuel Slaughter, the old church-

L

warden of St. Mark's, and was the mother of Mrs.
William Green of Richmond, of Mrs. Dr. Daniel
Green, of Sally C., wife of Rev. William Lockwood
of Md., of Marcia (Mrs. John B. Stanard). Elizabeth
Stanard *m.* Jno. Thompson, father of Fanny, wife of
Rev. John Cole, of Miss Eliza Thompson, and of Mrs.
Buffington. Jane, daughter of Edward of Blenheim *m.*
Major Bradford of the British army, father of Samuel
K. Bradford of the Revolution, whose son, Samuel
K. Bradford, vestryman of St. Mark's, *m.* Emily,
daughter of Samuel Slaughter (churchwarden of St.
Mark's), and was the father of S. S. Bradford, present
churchwarden; of Mrs. Gen. Wright, U. S. army;
of Mrs. Professor Nairne of Columbia College, New
York; of Dr. Robert B. Bradford, and of Mrs. Van
Schaik of New York City. William Champe Carter
of Farley, Culpeper County, sixth son of Edward of
Blenheim, *m.* Maria Farley, and their daughter Eliza
Hill *m.* Col. Samuel Storrow, the father of Mrs. Judge
Bell, of Mrs. Dr. Wm. Thompson, of Mrs. Weston,
of Mrs. Green, of Samuel and Farley. Charles
Carter of Cleve, son of King Carter by his second
wife Mary Landon, had a daughter Sarah who *m.*
William, a son of Rev. John Thompson of St. Mark's,
who was the father of Commodore Charles Carter
Byrd Thompson, U. S. navy, of Gilliss and of Wil-
liam Thompson.

THE CAVE FAMILY.

Among the members of the first vestry of St.
Mark's in 1731 was Benjamin Cave. I have in my
possession the original patent for 1000 acres of land
on the Rappidan (*sic*) River, to Abraham Bledsoe and

Benjamin Cave, "to be held in free and common socage, and not in capite or knight service, by paying yearly the free rent of one shilling for every fifty acres, on the feast of St. Michael the Archangel"; signed by William Gooch, Lieut.-Governor and Commander-in-Chief of the Colony and Dominion of Virginia. Done at Williamsburg, under the seal of the Colony, 28th September, 1728.

Benjamin Cave was vestryman of St. Mark's until 1740, when St. Thomas Parish was cut off from St. Mark's; and he and David Cave, who was Lay Reader at the old Orange Church near Ruckersville, became members of the new parish (St. Thomas) in Orange County, where they lived. The records of St. Thomas being lost, their relation to it cannot be traced. It is known, however, that the family adhered to the Church of their fathers; and one of the old ministers, about 1740, lived with Benjamin Cave, Sr., whose residence was within reach of the first chapel (near Brooking's) and the old Orange Church.

I have in my possession some original poems in MS., entitled "Spiritual Songs," written by a sister of Benjamin Cave, Sr., endorsed 1767. It is very pleasant to find one of these old-time church people, who some modern people think had no religion, giving utterance to her pious emotions in songs which are evidently the outpourings of a truly devotional spirit. It is said that Benjamin Cave used to repeat the church service from memory, chanting the psalms.

The first Benjamin Cave lived for a time at what is now known as Rhodes in Orange, and then moved to land on the Upper Rapidan near Cave's Ford, which derives its name from him.

Benjamin Cave represented Orange in the House
of Burgesses in 1756. He *m.* Hannah, *dau.* of Wm.
and sister of Abraham Bledsoe; *ch.* David, John,
Wm., Richard (who moved to Kentucky), Ann (to
North Carolina); Sally *m.* a Strother, Hannah *m.*
Capt. Mallory; *ch.* Elizabeth *m.* Oliver Welch.
Another daughter *m.* Capt. Robert Terrill, the father
of Mrs. Robert Lovell. Another daugher *m.* Oliver
Terrill, the father of Dr. Uriel Terrill, Delegate from
Orange. Another daughter *m.* Welch. William
Mallory *m.* Miss Gibson, and was the father of Robert
Mallory, late M. C. from Kentucky. Uriel Mallory
was the father of Mrs. John Taliaferro. Phil.
Mallory lived near Raccoon Ford. Elizabeth, *dau.*
of Benjamin Cave *m.* Col. Wm. Johnson; *ch.* 1. Valen-
tine *m.* Elizabeth Cave, *ch.* Belfield *m.* Miss Dickerson.
2. Fontaine *m.* Miss Duke. 3. Lucy *m.* Mr. Suggett.
4. Sally *m.* Mr. Dickerson. 5. Benjamin *m.* Miss
Barbour (see Barbour genealogy). 6. Col. Robert *m.*
Miss Suggett; *ch.* 1. Richard M., Vice-President and
hero of the "Thames"; 2. J. T. Johnson (M. C.);
3. James; 4. Benjamin. Benjamin Cave, son of first
Benjamin, *m.* a *dau.* of Dr. John Belfield of Richmond
County; *ch.* Belfield *m.* Miss Christy; *ch.* Belfield,
Clerk of Madison County, *m.* Miss Jones, and was
the father of Mrs. Governor Kemper. Emily *m.* Col.
Cave; Sally *m.* Shackleford; Hudson was Professor
at Chapel Hill, N. C.; Benjamin *m.* Miss Glassell
(father of Mrs. John Gray, Jr., of Traveller's Rest).
Benjamin, son of Benjamin and Elizabeth, *m.* Miss
White; *ch.* William, Belfield, John and Margaret, all
settled in Kentucky. Sarah, *dau.* of Benjamin, *m.*
Wm. Cassine; *ch.* Mary, who *m.* Mr. Taliaferro.
William, son of Benjamin and Elizabeth Cave, *m.*

Miss Smith; *ch.* John, William, and Hudson, settled
in Kentucky. Elizabeth *m.* John Bell, father of
Nelson H. Bell of Baltimore, who *m.* Hannah Cave.
Another *dau. m.* Mr. Irvine. Richard Cave *m.* Miss
Porter; *ch.* Thomas, Capt. William (father of Mrs.
Cornelia Thompson), Felix, Elizabeth, Mary, Cor-
nelia, Anne, and Hannah.

I am indebted to Mrs. Thompson for contributions
to the above notice.

THE CLAYTONS.

The first person of this name who appears in the
history of Virginia was the Rev. John Clayton, who
had been Rector of Crofton in Yorkshire. In 1683
he addressed to the Royal Society in England, at
their request, several letters giving an account of
what he calls "Several Observables" in Virginia.
These letters discuss the soil, climate, natural history
and agriculture of the colony of that day. They
display great acuteness of observation, fulness of
learning, and practical suggestions. He seems to
have been the first to point out the value of marl and
muck as fertilizers, and suggest to the planters the
advantages of draining the tidewater swamps. And
when his opinion was laughed at and rejected by the
overseers, he went to work and put them to shame
by laying dry a pond of water, bringing to the light
of the sun an inexhaustible soil.

The next man of mark of this name was the Rev.
David Clayton, minister of Blissland Parish, New
Kent Co., Virginia, from 1704 to 1724. In his
parochial reports to the Bishop of London he says
(1724) that his Parish was sixty miles long, that he

had under his charge 136 families and about seventy communicants.

There is John Clayton at Williamsburg, Attorney General, and a friend of Spotswood, who accompanied Mr. Fontaine in the first trip to Germanna in 1714. There was also a Clayton a vestryman and justice in Essex Co. The family tradition is that Major Philip Clayton came to Culpeper from New Kent through Essex. What was his precise relation to the foregoing clergymen is not certainly known. His name first appears in our church records in the year 1741, when he was chosen vestryman of St. Mark's, and a patent for land from Lord Fairfax to John Brown (now before us) is endorsed as having been surveyed by Philip Clayton, 1749. He was the deputy, doing all the duties of the office for Roger Dixon, Clerk of Culpeper, who lived in the lower country. He married Ann, sister of Robert Coleman, on whose land the courthouse was built. He had one son, Samuel (his successor in the vestry), who married his cousin Ann Coleman, and among their children were Major Philip Clayton the second, an officer of the Revolution, whose daughter Sarah Ann married Dr. James B. Wallace.

Nancy, sister of the last Philip, and daughter of Samuel, married Jeremiah Strother, and was the grandmother of the Rev. J. S. Hansbrough, and Mrs. Judge Williams of Orange C. H., Colonel Woodson Hansbrough, and Mrs. Waldridge.

Lucy, daughter of the first Philip, married William Williams (vestryman), and their children were Major John, General James, both officers in the Revolution, Philip of Woodstock, William Clayton of Richmond, Mrs. Stevens and Mrs. Green. (See Williams genealogy).

Susan, another daughter of the first Philip, married Colonel James Slaughter, father of Captain Philip Slaughter. (See Slaughter genealogy).

Another daughter married Nathaniel Pendleton, brother of Judge Edmund Pendleton, President of the Court of Appeals (see Pendleton genealogy). Another daughter married a Crittenden, and was the mother (I believe) of Senator Crittenden of Kentucky.

Major Philip Clayton the elder lived at Catalpa, so named from a Catalpa tree he transplanted from Essex, the first of its kind in the county.

Philip Clayton went from Virginia to Georgia, where he died, and was buried at Sand Hills, near the city of Augusta. His children were first, George Roots of Milledgeville, cashier of State Bank and treasurer of the State, highly honored and esteemed. 2. Augustine Smith Clayton, of Athens, graduated at Franklin College, distinguished at the bar, Judge of the Western Circuit, and Member of Congress, where he won a national reputation. He was an able statesman, jurist, and man of letters, and left his impress upon the policy and literature of the State. He died a Christian, on 1st of June, 1839, in the 56th year of his age, leaving nine children, viz. George Roots, Augustine Smith, Wm. Wirt, Cashier Merchants Bank, Atlanta; Philip, consul at Callao, and churchwarden, St. Paul's, Greensboro, died 1877; Almyra; Dallas; Edward P., cotton factor and commission merchant of Augusta, and churchwarden of St. Paul's; Julia; Claudia, and Augusta.

THE COLEMANS.

Robert Coleman, 1st of the name in Culpeper, *m.* Sarah Ann Saunders. The town of Fairfax (Culpeper) was founded on fifty acres of his land in 1759.

He had one son, Robert, who emigrated to Kentucky and *m.* Mrs. Thompson, a sister of Major Philip Lightfoot.

Gilly, *dau.* of the 1st Robert and Miss Saunders, *m.* General Edward Stevens, the Revolutionary hero and elector, who cast the vote of the district for Washington, and whose son John *m.* Polly, *dau.* of the 1st William Williams.

Ann, 2d *dau.* of 1st Robert, *m.* Samuel Clayton. (See Clayton genealogy.)

Rosa, 3d *dau.*, *m.* Foster of Tennessee, one of whose *ch.* was the Senator in Congress from that State.

Another *dau.* of 1st Robert *m.* Col. John Slaughter, son of the 1st Francis of that name.

Another *dau.* *m.* Francis Slaughter, brother of the foregoing John. (See Slaughter genealogy.)

Another *dau.* *m.* a Yancey.

Lucy, another *dau.*; *m.* French Strother, so long representative of Culpeper in the General Assembly and in the Convention of 1775–6, and whose oldest *dau.* P. French was first wife of Capt. P. Slaughter. (See Slaughter genealogy.)

The 8th *dau.* of 1st Robert *m.* a Crutcher, and one of their daughters *m.* a Foushee.

Robert Coleman, in his will (1793) recorded in Culpeper, leaves legacies to his daughters Ann Clayton, Sarah Slaughter, Lucy Strother, Francis Crutcher and Susanna Yancey. Philip Clayton was his executor.

THE CONWAY FAMILY.

This family has been identified with the Episcopal Church from the earliest times. You may trace the name through the vestry-books from the first settlements in the Northern Neck to the present time. I have in my possession the will of Edwin Conway, dated 19th of March, 1698. In the grave-yard of Whitechapel, Lancaster County, there is a tombstone of Mary Ball, daughter of Edwin Conway, and one of James Ball, her husband, who was a near relative of Gen. Washington's grandfather, who was the son of Col. Wm. Ball, the first of the name who came from England in 1650 and settled at the mouth of Corotoman River. I transfer from the will the following clauses : — "First and *principally*, I bequeath my soul to the God that gave it, in certain hope, notwithstanding my unworthiness, to receive pardon of all my sins, through the blessed merits of my dear Redeemer; and by no other way or means do I hope for pardon. My body I commit to be buried in my burying-ground at Lancaster, by the left side of my dear wife Sarah, in certain hope, thro' the merits aforesaid, that soul and body will have a joyful meeting at the resurrection of the just." He gives to his son Francis and to his heirs lawfully begotten 706 acres of land in Essex; to the child or children "whereof my wife now goeth withal" the crop of sweet-scented tobacco on the lower plantation. To his son Edwin all the lands in Lancaster given him by deed, with his mathematical books and instruments, and all "the cloth and stuff sent for to England." He appoints his friend Andrew Jackson, Reuben Conway and H. Thacker to be *overseers* of his will, desiring them to carefully advise and instruct his children in their persons and estates and to be assistants to his dear wife.

The aforesaid E. Conway married Elizabeth Thompson. Their son Francis, near Port Royal, Caroline, married Rebecca, daughter of Jno. Catlett and Elizabeth Grimes. (This John Catlett was son of the John Catlett killed by the Indians while defending the fort at Port Royal.) Nelly, daughter of Francis and granddaughter of Edwin Conway, married James Madison, Sr., and was the mother of President Madison, who was born at Port Conway, opposite to Port Royal, where his mother was visiting, at 12 o'clock at night between the 5th and 6th of March, 1751, and was baptized the 31st of March by the Rev. Wm. Davis, and had for godfathers John Moore and Jonathan Gibson, and for godmothers Mrs. Rebecca Moore and Misses Judith and Elizabeth Catlett.

The author of this will was the great-grandfather of old Capt. Catlett Conway, of Hawfield, in Orange (now owned by Wm. Crenshaw, Esq.,) who was the father of the late Francis, Catlett, John, and Henry Conway, of Orange and Madison; of Mrs. Hay Taliaferro, of Rose Hill, Orange County, and of Mrs. Fitzhugh, of Bedford, King George. Dr. Charles Conway (vestryman) is a direct descendant of the old vestryman, the first Edwin Conway of Lancaster.

THE FIELDS.

The first person of the name in the parish register is Henry Field, Sr., a member of the first vestry chosen by the freeholders and housekeepers of St.

Mark's Parish, at Germanna, in January 1731. The next is Abraham Field, elected vestryman at the Great Fork Church in 1744, and served till his death in 1774, a term of thirty years. He had a son John, who represented Culpeper in the House of Burgesses in 1765. He was probably the Col. John Field who had served in Braddock's War, and who fell, fighting gallantly at the head of his regiment, at the battle of Point Pleasant. One of his daughters married Lawrence Slaughter, an officer of the Revolution, and who was the father of John Field Slaughter, who married Miss Alexander of Prince William. Another of Col. John Field's daughters married Col. George Slaughter, who raised one of the first companies of minute-men in Culpeper; and after the war moved to Kentucky with George Rogers Clarke, commanded a fort at the Falls of the Ohio, and was one of the founders of the city of Louisville, which was then in the State of Virginia.

Henry Field, Sr., the vestryman of 1731, served in that office and as churchwarden till 1762, a term of thirty-one years. He executed many commissions for the vestry, such as going to Williamsburg on horseback several times on their behalf, and paying quit-rents for the churches and glebes. He and Francis Slaughter and Robert Green chose a site for a chapel between Shaw's Mountain, the Devil's Run and Hazel River. He was succeeded in the vestry by Henry Field, Jr., who served till his removal from the parish of St. Mark's into Bromfield Parish, whose records are lost or we should probably have found his name on the vestry-books there. He represented Culpeper in the Convention at Williamsburg in 1774 to consider the state of the country, in the

House of Burgesses in 1775, and with French
Strother in the Convention of 1776 which asserted
the principle of religious liberty, declared American
independence, and adopted the first Constitution.
Henry Field, Jr., died in 1785, leaving six sons—
Daniel, Henry, George, Joseph, Thomas and John,
who were the ancestors of the families of that name.
The late judge of this court, Richard H. Field, and
his brothers Yancey and Stanton, were the sons of
Daniel Field of what is now Madison. He (the
Judge) married first Matilda, daughter of Robert
Slaughter of the Grange, and second Philippa,
daughter of the Honorable Philip P. Barbour. His
three sons were killed in battle during the late war,
and his daughter (Mrs. Norvell) is the only surviving
child. Gen. James Field of the Culpeper bar, who
lost a limb at the battle of Slaughter's Mountain, is
a son of Yancey Field. He married Miss Cowherd
of Orange.

THE FRY FAMILY.

The ancestor of the Frys who once so abounded
in Culpeper, was Col. Joshua Fry, an Englishman
educated at Oxford. He lived some time in Essex,
was Professor of Mathematics at William and Mary
College, a member of the House of Burgesses, com-
missioner to run one of the lines between Virginia
and North Carolina, and negotiator of the treaty
of Logstown. He, with Peter Jefferson, made a map
of Virginia in 1749. He commanded a regiment
against the French and Indians, of which Washington was lieutenant-colonel. I am indebted to his
lineal descendant Francis Fry, of Charlottesville, for

a copy of his commission, from the original in **Mr.** Fry's possession :—

"To JOSHUA FRYE.

"His Majesty, by his royal instructions, commanded me to send a proper number of forces to erect and maintain a fort at the Monongahela and Ohio Rivers; and having a good opinion of your loyalty, conduct and ability, I do hereby institute, appoint and commission you to be Colonel and Commander-in-chief of the forces now raising, to be called the Virginia Regiment, with which and the cannon, arms and ammunition, necessary provisions and stores, you are with all possible dispatch to proceed to said fork of Monongahela, and there act according to your instructions."

Col. Joshua Fry married Mrs. Hill, the daughter of Paul Micon, a French Huguenot physican. He was the father of the Rev. Henry Fry, who lived in the fork of Crooked Run and the Robinson River, and occasionally preached in the Episcopal church near Orange C. H. when they had no minister, always prefacing his sermons with the old church service, says Col. Frank Taylor, a vestryman of that church. He was one of those good and guileless men whom all Christians respected and loved. His son Reuben *m.* Ann *dau.* of Col. James Slaughter, and their. *ch.* were Judge Joseph Fry, of Wheeling, Henry, Senator of Kanawha, and Philip S., late clerk of Orange and father of Philip, present clerk, William, Thomas and Luther. Thomas W., son of Rev. H. Fry, *m.* 1st Mrs. Slaughter, whose maiden name was Bourn, and 2d Ann *dau.* of Col. Abram Maury of Madison. He with three *ch.* moved to Kentucky (1816). Joshua *m.* Miss Walker, and Mrs. Willis *dau.* of William Twyman. Hugh and Joshua Fry, of Richmond, were his sons. Henry *m.* Mildred

M

dau. of Rev. Mat Maury. Frank Fry, Sr., of Char-
lottesville, is their son. John *m.* Miss Heywood, of
Culpeper, and lived at the Warm Springs. Mrs.
Dr. Archer Strother was his *dau.* Wesley *m.* 1st
Miss Walker, and 2d a French lady, Miss Leflet, and
had thirteen children. Thornton *m.* a *dau.* of Hon.
Philip R. Thompson, and their *ch.* were Gen. Burkitt
Fry, C. S. A., Dr. Frank and Mrs. Jno. L. Bacon, of
Richmond. Margaret *dau.* of Rev. Henry *m.* Philip
Lightfoot and moved to Kentucky. Martha *m.*
Goodrich Lightfoot and had ten *ch.*, of whom Edward
Lightfoot, of Madison, is the only survivor. Maria
m. Hugh Walker and went to Kentucky, and had
many children.

Col. Joshua Fry, the head of this family in Vir-
ginia, patented 1000 acres of land on the Robinson
River in 1726, and 400 acres "in the fork of the
Robinson" in 1739. Charles Meriwether Fry, of the
Bank of New York, who *m.* Miss Leigh, is the son of
Belville, who was the son of Joshua, who was the
son of Rev. Henry Fry.

THE GARNETT FAMILY.

The chief seat of this family in Virginia was the
county of Essex, where many of this name occupied
a high social position and filled many places of public
trust. The Hon. James M. Garnett was a member
of Congress from 1805 to 1809. The Hon. Robert S.
Garnett was in Congress from 1817 to 1827. The
Hon. Muscoe Garnett was also a member of Congress
and of the State Convention of 1850. Dr. A. Y. P.
Garnett, who married the daughter of Governor
Wise, has been for many years a leading medical

man of Washington City. There was a General Garnett of the Confederate army who fell in battle, whose sister married Professor Williamson of the Virginia Military Institute; and there is now a Professor Garnett in the college at Annapolis, Md.

I have been disappointed in receiving the information which would have enabled me to show the connecting links between these several members of the family in Virginia. The first of the name in Culpeper was Anthony Garnett, who came from Essex, and from the names James, Muscoe and Reuben, which are common to both families, they probably sprang from the same stock. Anthony Garnett was a vestryman, churchwarden and lay reader of St. Mark's Parish from 1758. He lived at the Horse Shoe, where Joseph Wilmer, Jr., now resides, and when there was no minister of the parish, was in the habit of burying the dead with the church service. He married Mrs. Bowler (Miss Jones), and his children were Robin, who moved to Kentucky and died in his ninety-eighth year. His daughter married Stokely Towles of Madison, and their daughter married James L. Waggener of Russelville, Ky., father of Professor Waggener, of Bethel College, Ky. James, son of Anthony, was minister of Crooked Run Church. He married Miss Rowe, and was the father of Edmund, who was the father of the late Rev. James Garnett, whose sons, Joel, Absalom and Franklin, and daughter Tabitha, still survive. James, Sr., was the father of the present James, whose children are Muscoe and others. John, son of Anthony, moved to Kentucky. Thomas married Miss Hawkins. Reuben, son of Anthony, married Miss Twyman, and was the father of the venerable Miss Tabitha Garnett, who, like her namesake in the Bible, is kind to the poor. Lucy married a Tinsley, Sally married a Stepp, and Betsy married William Willis of Culpeper, the father of the late Isaac Willis, who has many descendants, among whom is the Rev. John C. Willis of Indian Town, Orange County.

THE GLASSELL FAMILY.

The Glassell (originally Glassele) family went from Poictiers, France, with Mary Queen of Scots on her return to her native country. John Glassell of Runkan, Scotland, m. Mary Coalter, a warm Covenanter, and their son Robert m. Mary Kelton, and their son Andrew Glassell was born at Galway, Dumfriesshire, Scotland, near Torthorwald, "Castle of the Douglass," Oct. 8th, 1738, and emigrated to Madison County, Virginia, in 1756. He imported mechanics from Scotland, and built a large brick residence on his fine estate on the upper Robinson River, known as Torthorwald. He m. (1776) Elizabeth dau. of Erasmus Taylor of Orange County, and died July 4th, 1827, aged 89. Their children were—

1. Millie Glassell m. Reuben Smith. Issue 1. Jane m. in 1822 Hon. Jeremiah Morton (M. C.); issue one son, died in infancy, and one daughter, Mildred m. J. J. Halsey, issue 1. Fannie M.; 2. Anna Augusta (Mrs. Alexander); 3. J. Morton m. Miss Stearns; 4. R. Ogden m. Miss Walker, and 5. Joseph J. Halsey.

2. George A. Smith (now of Bell County, Texas), m. Julia dau. of James Somerville of Culpeper Co.; issue 1. Eudora G. (Mrs. Lees); 2. Jane M. (Mrs. Ware); 3. Mary S. (Mrs. Coffee); 4. Margaret (Mrs.

Russell), and several sons unmarried. 3. Dr. William
R. Smith (late of Galveston), *m.* first Mrs. Middleton,
no issue; *m.* second Mary Mayrant, issue John M.
m. Miss Terry, and Mildred (Mrs. Crosby of New
York City).

2. John Glassell *m.* first Louisa Brown. Issue 1.
Dr. Andrew *m.* Miss Downing; 2. Fanny (Mrs. Ware);
3. Mary (Mrs. Conway); 4. Louisa (Mrs. Eno of
Pennsylvania). John Glassell *m.* second Mrs. Lee,
née Margaret Scott; issue Mildred S. (Mrs. Covell)
and John *m.* Miss Thom. John Glassell *m.* third
Mary Ashton, by whom no issue.

3. Mary Kelton Glassell *m.* Michael Wallace. Issue
1. Ellen (Mrs. Somerville); 2. Gustavus; 3. H.
Nelson; 4. Elizabeth (Mrs. Wallace); 5. Louisa (Mrs.
Goodwin); 6. James, and 7. Marianna (Mrs. Conway).

4. Helen Buchan Glassell *m.* Daniel Grinnan. Issue
1. Robert A. *m.* Robertine Temple; 2. Cornelia (died
1864); 3. Andrew G. *m.* George S. Bryan; 4. Daniella M.

5. Jane M. Glassell *m.* Benjamin Cave. (See Cave
genealogy.)

6. Major James M. Glassell, U. S. Army, *m.* Eudora
Swartout.

7. Andrew Glassell *m.* Susan Thornton. Issue 1.
Andrew *m.* Miss Toland; 2. Capt. William S. Glassell;
3. Susan S. *m.* first Colonel George S. Patton (see
Williams genealogy); *m.* second George H. Smith of
California.

8. William E. Glassell *m* first Margaret Somerville.
Issue one child living, Margaret (Mrs. Weeks of
Louisiana). *M.* second Harriet Scott.

John Glassell, brother of Andrew, came to Fredericksburg long before the Revolution. He was a merchant of large transactions, having branch establishments in Culpeper and Fauquier, and became very rich. He returned to Scotland before the Revolution. He married Helen Buchan, of the family of the Earl of Buchan. One of her sisters married an Erskine, and another Dalhousie; and Lord Erskine and the Earl of Dalhousie were her nephews. John Glassell's only daughter, Johanna, married Lord Campbell, who became Duke of Argyle, and the present Duke of Argyle is her son.

GENEALOGY OF THE GREEN FAMILY.

Robert Green, the first of the family who came to this country (son of William, an Englishman, an officer in the body-guard of William, Prince of Orange), arrived here about the year 1712, and settled with his uncle, William Duff, a Quaker, in King George County. He was born in the year 1695. When a young man he married Eleanor Dunn, of Scotland, and settled in Culpeper, in St. Mark's Parish, near what is now Brandy, a station on the Washington City and Virginia Midland Railroad. He had seven sons: William, Robert, Duff, John, Nicholas, James and Moses.

1. William *m.* Miss Coleman of Caroline, died in Culpeper County and left eight children.

2. Robert *m.* Patty Ball of Northumberland, died in Culpeper and left five children.

3. Duff *m.* first Miss Thomas, *m.* second Miss Willis, left five children. Gen. Duff Green of Washington City was his grandson.

4. John (Col. John Green of the Revolution) *m.* Susanna Blackwell; issue, 1. William *m.* Lucy

Williams, issue, one child to live, John W. Green, Judge of the Court of Appeals of Virginia. Judge Green *m.* first Mary Browne; issue, 1. William Green (the eminent lawyer) *m.* Columbia, daughter of Samuel Slaughter of Culpeper; issue, John, killed in battle in 1863, and Bettie (Mrs. Hayes of Fredericksburg). 2. Raleigh B. Green died unmarried. 3. Dr. Daniel S. Green, formerly of the U. S. Navy, *m.* Virginia, daughter of Samuel Slaughter of Culpeper; issue, Dr. Wm. Green, Professor in Baltimore Medical College, Mollie (Mrs. Morton of Baltimore), and Samuel Green, a lawyer at Charlestown, West Virginia. Judge Green *m.* second Miss Cooke (a granddaughter of George Mason, author of the Virginia Bill of Rights); issue, 1. John C. Green (for twenty years Commonwealth's Attorney for Culpeper) *m.* Lucy, daughter of Dr. George Morton of Culpeper; 2. Thomas C. Green (Judge of the Court of Appeals of West Virginia) *m.* Miss McDonald; 3. George M. Green *m.* Miss Ashby of Fauquier; 4. James W. Green (a lawyer at Culpeper) *m.* Miss McDonald; 5. Lucy W. Green died unmarried.

2. John, second son of Col. John Green, was killed in a duel, at 18 years of age, at Valley Forge.

3. Robert, third son of Col. John Green, *m.* Miss Edmunds, had two children — a son and a daughter; son left no children; daughter *m.* Robert Payne, lived in Nicholas County, Kentucky, had children.

4. Duff, fourth son of Col. John Green, died young.

5. George, fifth son, died an infant.

6. Moses, sixth son of Col. John Green, *m.* Fanny Richards; issue, 1. John died at 22 years of age; 2. Julia *m.* Bernard Peyton; issue, Green Peyton *m.* a daughter of Dr. Charles Carter of Charlottesville,

and Thomas Jefferson Peyton *m.* a daughter of Bishop Johns; 3. Thomas Green (now of Washington City) *m.* first Miss Lyons, *m.* second Miss Ritchie, *m.* third Miss Lomax. His children are Mary (Mrs. Stone of Washington City) and Thomas Ritchie Green; 4. William Green *m.* Miss Saunders, has children; 5. A. Magill Green *m.* Miss Farish, had children.

7. Thomas, seventh son of Col. John Green, *m.* first Miss Miller; issue, Edward H. *m.* first Miss Short, *m.* second Miss Ward. Thomas Green *m.* second Lucy Peyton of Stafford County, Va., and moved to Christian County, Kentucky; issue:

1. Ann Augusta Green *m.* Edward Randolph; issue, Bathurst E. Randolph *m.* Lizzie Glass, and Dr. Thomas G. Randolph *m.* Anne Edgar.

2. Lucy Williams Green *m.* first Daniel Henry; issue, 1. Lucy Ann *m.* John Nelson, 2. Mary Green *m.* George Champlin (a lawyer at Hopkinsville, Ky.) 3. Dr. Green Henry *m.* Kate Mansfield. Lucy Williams Henry *m.* second James C. Moore; issue, 1. Lucy W. *m.* Charles Dade, 2. Mattie P., 3. James C., 4. Gustavus H.

3. Mary Peyton Green *m.* first Thomas Edmunds; issue, John T. Edmunds *m.* Mollie Campbell. Mary Peyton Edmunds *m.* second Col. William S. Moore, of Alabama; issue, 1. James H., 2. Lucy Peyton *m.* Ecksteine Norton, of New York city, 3. Lizzie McA. *m.* John D. Tyler, 4. William S., 5. Fannie Peyton, 6. Caroline Green.

4. John R. Green *m.* Elizabeth Nelson, issue 1. William *m.* Miss Armstead, 2. Wallace *m.* Miss Somerville, 3. Edward *m.* Miss Hartman, 4. Lucius *m.* in California, 5. John R. *m.* Miss Phelps, 6. Rosalie *m.*

Hunter Wood (a lawyer at Hopkinsville, Ky., and district attorney) 7. Lizzie *m.* Nicholas Edmunds, 8. Anna *m.* William T. Townes, 9. Robert, 10, Nelson.

5. Thomas Green *m.* first Caroline Venable, issue Lucy P. *m.* Randolph Dade, 2. Bettie *m.* Bankhead Dade, 3. George *m.* Lizzie Dade, 4. John R. Thomas Green *m.* second Mary T. Moore, issue 5. Thomas, 6. James.

8. Elizabeth, daughter of Col. John Green *m.* John Hove, of Fauquier County, no issue.

Nicholas, the fifth son of Robert Green, *m.* Miss Price, had a number of children who moved to Kentucky.

James, the sixth son of Robert Green, *m.* E. Jones, issue 1. Gabriel *m.* Miss Grant, moved to Kentucky on Green River, 2. James *m.* Miss Jones, issue Jones, James, Strother, Charles, Duff and others (Mrs. Howard Shackelford, now of Charlottesville, is a daughter of Jones, and Col. John Shackelford Green, a gallant officer in the late war, is a son of James), 3. Duff died a bachelor, 4. Jones *m.* Miss Neville, 5. Robert *m.* Miss Edmunds, 6. John *m.* Miss Catlett, of Fauquier, moved to Henderson Co., Ky., 7. Dolly *m.* Nimrod Turner, 8. Elizabeth *m.* W. Peacock, died in England, 9. Lucy *m.* a Glasscock, moved to Missouri, 10. Polly *m.* a Catlett, 11. Austin *m.* Miss Ball, moved to Kentucky.

Moses, the seventh son of Robert Green, *m.* Miss Blackwell (sister of Susanna), issue two daughters, 1. Sally died without issue, 2. Eleanor *m.* Gen. James Williams, issue 1. William *m.* Miss Stubblefield, 2. James died single, 3. Sally *m.* George Strother, member of Congress from the Culpeper district (see Strother and Williams genealogies).

There has been a continuous succession of vestry-men in this family, from Robert of 1731, who was a member of the House of Burgesses, to Major J. W. Green, now a leading member of the Culpeper bar.

THE LIGHTFOOTS.

The Lightfoots were among the early colonists in Virginia. They seem to have settled originally in Gloucester and James City, when the latter embraced what is now Charles City County. Colonel Philip Lightfoot was a vestryman of Petsworth Parish as early as 1683. By his last will he devised his lands to his eldest son Francis, remainder to his son Philip. Francis devised his lands to his daughter Elizabeth, who married Peter Randolph of Henrico; remainder to his brother Philip Lightfoot. The entail was docked by the House of Burgesses in 1740, and by agreement between the parties these lands were vested in Philip Lightfoot.

The present writer remembers to have seen at Sandy Point in Charles City, when it was owned and occupied by Col. Robert B. Bolling, divers portraits of the old Lightfoots. There were three William Lightfoots in succession at Sandy Point, and their tombs are still there. The first died in 1727, the second in 1809, and the third in 1810. We have in our possession now a copy of Bayles' folio dictionary, in ten volumes, with the name and coat-of-arms of William Lightfoot Tedington on each volume. Tedington was one of the four farms which composed the splendid estate of Sandy Point, between the James and Chickahominy Rivers. Three of these farms were inherited by Miss Minge (Mrs. Robert B. Bolling), and the fourth was added by Mr. Bolling.

There is a family of Lightfoots at Port Royal, Caroline, represented by the late Philip Lightfoot and his sons, Lewis Lightfoot and his brother John.

In 1726 we find the name of Major Goodrich Lightfoot as a member of the vestry of St. George's Parish, Spotsylvania, when that parish and county embraced what was afterwards the parish of St. Mark's and county of Culpeper. He was one of the lay readers at the Germanna Church, and he and Robert Slaughter were appointed to count all the tobacco plants from the mouth of the Rapidan to the mouth of Mountain Run, and up Mountain Run and across to the mouth of the Robinson River, in obedience to an Act of the Assembly limiting the number of plants to be cultivated by each planter.

At the organization of St. Mark's Parish, at Germanna in 1731, he was chosen a member of the first vestry by the freeholders and housekeepers of St. Mark's, his home being within the limits of the new parish. He served as vestryman and churchwarden till his death in 1738, and was succeeded by Captain Goodrich Lightfoot in 1741, who served till his removal from the parish in 1771. William Lightfoot was also a vestryman from 1752 to 1758, when he moved out of its bounds to the parish of Bromfield, which had been cut off from St. Mark's in 1752. William, we think, was the father of Goodrich, who married the daughter of the Rev. Henry Fry, who lived in the fork of Crooked Run and the Robinson River. Goodrich Lightfoot lived opposite to the present home of George Clark, Esq., on the Robinson River. He was the brother of the late Major Philip Lightfoot of the Culpeper bar, and of Walker Lightfoot (clerk), and he was the father of Frank Lightfoot, clerk of Culpeper, who married Miss Fielder (father of Col. Charles E. Lightfoot), and of Edward of Madison, who married Miss Conner, and is the father of Virginia; and John, who married Miss Turner, the granddaughter of Major John Roberts of the Revolution, whose wife was the daughter of the old vestryman Captain Robert Pollard.

From the names of Philip, John, and William, which were common to these several branches of the Lightfoots, the presumption is that they sprang from the same stock.

THE MADISON FAMILY.

From the record of James Madison, Sr., the father of the President, and from the record of James Madison, Jr., the President.

The first of the name in Virginia, John Madison, patented land in Gloucester County in 1653. His son John was the father of Ambrose, who married Frances, daughter of James Taylor, Aug. 29th, 1721. Their son, James Madison, Sr., was married to Nelly, daughter of Francis Conway of Caroline, Sept. 13th, 1749. James Madison, Jr., (the President) was born at Port Conway at 12 o'clock (midnight) 6th March, 1751, was baptized by Rev. Wm. Davis, March 31st, and had for godfathers John Moore and Jonathan Gibson, and for godmothers Mrs. Rebecca Moore and Misses Judith and Elizabeth Catlett. Frances, daughter of James, Sr., born June 18th, 1753, baptized by the Rev. Mungo Marshall, July 31st; godfathers, Richard Beale and Erasmus Taylor; godmothers, Miss Milly Taylor and Mrs. Frances Beale. Ambrose, son of James, Sr., born Jan. 27th,

1756, baptized by Rev. Mr. Marshall, March 2d; godfathers, James Coleman and George Taylor; godmothers, Mrs. Jane Taylor and Alice Chew. Catlett, son of James, Sr., born Feb. 10th, 1758, baptized by Rev. James Maury, Feb. 22d; godfathers, Col. Wm. Taliaferro and Richard Beale; godmothers, Mrs. E. Beale and Miss Milly Chew. Nelly, daughter of James, Sr., (Mrs. Hite) born Feb. 14th, 1760, baptized March 6th by Rev. Wm. Giberne; godfathers, Larkin Chew and William Moore; godmothers, Miss E. Catlett and Miss C. Bowie. William Madison born May 1st, 1762, baptized May 23d by Rev. James Marye, Jr.; godfathers, William Moore and James Taylor; godmothers, Miss Mary Willis and Miss Milly Chew. Sarah (Mrs. Thomas Macon), born Aug. 17th, 1764, baptized Sept. 15th, by Rev. James Marye; godfathers, Captain R. J. Barbour and Andrew Shepherd; godmothers, Mrs. Sarah Taylor and Miss Mary Conway. Elizabeth Madison born Feb. 19th, 1768, baptized Feb. 22d by Rev. Thos. Martin; godfathers, Major T. Burnley and Ambrose Powell; godmothers, Miss Alice and Miss Nelly Chew. Reuben Madison born Sept. 19th, 1771, baptized Nov. 10th by Rev. Mr. Barnett; godfathers, Francis Barbour and James Chew; godmothers, Alice and Nelly Chew. Frances Taylor Madison (Mrs. Dr. Robert Rose) born Oct. 9th, 1774, baptized Oct. 30th by Rev. Mr. Wingate; godfathers, Thomas Bell and Richard Taylor; godmothers, Miss Frances Taylor and Miss Elizabeth Taylor. Here the old family record closes. It is a model record, which others would do well to imitate. In it we have the succession of the ministers of the parish, Wingate being the last of the colonial clergy.

N

James Madison, Jr., was chairman of the Committee of Public Safety and an active vestryman.

The living representatives of James Madison, Sr., so far as is known by the writer, are:

1. The oldest child (Nelly) of Ambrose, eldest son of James Madison, Sr., married Dr. Willis, and their living descendants are Col. John Willis of Orange and his children.

2. Of General William Madison, 2d brother of James Madison, Jr., (President) the living descendants are Wm. Madison and children of Texas, Dr. James Madison of Orange, and the children of Col. John Willis through their mother; the wife and children of Wm. P. Dabney of Powhatan; the children of Robert Marye; the wife and children of Dorsey Taliaferro of Texas; the children of Major John H. Lee by his second wife Fanny, daughter of Lewis Willis and Eliza Madison; Dr. Robert Madison (the son of Robert) and his children, Virginia Military Institute; the children of Daniel F. Slaughter by his first wife, Letitia Madison; and the children of Dr. Thomas T. Slaughter by his first wife.

Of Frank, third brother of the President, the representatives are the children of Alexander and Thompson Shepherd.

The eldest sister of the President, Nelly (Mrs. Hite), left a son and daughter. Her son, Madison Hite, left two sons and a daughter (Mrs. Baker), all believed to be living. Her daughter Nelly married Dr. Baldwin. Miss Baldwin, the untiring Missionary in Greece, and now at Joppa, is the illustrious offspring of this marriage.

The second sister of the President, Sarah, married

Thomas Macon. Of a number of children of this marriage, two only left issue. 1. Conway Macon left a son and three daughters. The son, who was killed at Manassas, left an only son, Edgar, now living. Conway Macon's daughters married Washington, Cave and Smith; the first and last of whom are living and have several children. 2. James Madison Macon's daughters, Mrs. Hite and Mrs. Knox. There was also a Thomas Macon, Jr., and that mother in Israel, the late Mrs. Reuben Conway, was a daughter of Thomas Macon, Sr., and Sarah Madison.

The youngest sister of the President, Fanny, married Dr. Robert Rose and they emigrated to Tennessee about 1822 or '23, with children, Ambrose, Hugh, James, Robert, Erasmus, Henry, Sam, Nelly, Frances and Mary. Of these, Dr. Erasmus Rose, if living, is a resident of Memphis.

James Madison, Sr., the zealous old vestryman, had a habit of making short sketches of sermons he heard. Col. John Willis had some of them. His great son, the President, left among his papers comments on the Gospels and the Acts of the Apostles. Among these are the following:—"Christ's Divinity appears in St. John, ch. xx. v. 28." On the words of Christ to St. Paul, "Arise and go into the city, and it shall be told thee what thou shalt do," his comment is, "It is not the talking, but the walking and working person, that is the true Christian." It was he that furnished a list of theological authors for the Library of the University of Virginia. There are doubtless other descendants of James Madison, Sr., but the author of this notice is unable to trace the line of their connection with him.

THE PENDLETON FAMILY.

The Pendleton family of Virginia deduce descent from Henry Pendleton of Norwich, England, whose two sons, Nathaniel (Minister of the Established Church of England, died without issue) and Philip[1] emigrated to the colony in 1674, and settled in that portion of New Kent County which now forms Caroline County.

Philip[1] *b.* 1650, visited England in 1680, returning *m.*, 1682, Isabella Hurt, *d.* 1721; issue:

i. Elizabeth[2] *m.* Samuel Clayton of Caroline County; issue, Philip[3] of "Catalpa." (See Clayton genealogy.)

ii. Rachel[2] *m.* John Vass.

iii. Catherine[2] *m.* John Taylor; issue, "John[3] Taylor of Caroline," U. S. S., &c.

iv. Henry[2] *b.* 1683, *m.* 1701, Mary *dau.* of James Taylor, *b.* 1688. He *d.* May, 1721, his wife surviving him *m.* 2d Ed. Watkins and *d.* 1770.

v. Isabella[2] *m.* Richard Thomas, from whom were descended Gov. James and Judge Philip Pendleton Barbour of Orange County.

vi. John[2] *b.* 1691, removed to Amherst Co., *m.* —— Tinsley of Madison Co.; he *d.* 1775. Descendants in Amherst, Hanover and other counties.

vii. Philip[2] *b.*   , *m.* Elizabeth Pollard.

Issue of Henry[2] and Mary (Taylor) Pendleton:

i. James[3] *b.* 1702, *d.* 1761; *m.* ——; issue, James[4], Henry[4], Philip[4] and Anne[4] *m.* —— Taylor.

ii. Philip[3] *m.* and dying 1778, left 15 children, who intermarried with the Gaines, Barbours, Turners, &c.

iii. Nathaniel[3] *b.* 1715, *m.* —— his second cousin, *dau.* of Philip Clayton; he *d.* 1794, in Culpeper Co., Va.

iv. John[3] *b.* 1719, *m.* and dying April, 1799, left daughters. Descendants in King William and King and Queen Counties.

v. Edmund[3] *b.* September 9, 1721, *d.* Richmond, Va., October 23, 1803; patriot and jurist; *m.* twice; 1st, Jan. 1741, Elizabeth Roy who *d.* in Nov. following; 2d, June 1743, Sarah Pollard. There are on record in the Virginia Land Registry Office grants in his name numbering nearly 10,000 acres of land.

vi. Mary[3] *m.* —— Gaines.

vii. Isabella[3] *m.* —— Gaines. She was the grandmother of Gen. Edmund Pendleton Gaines, U. S. A.

James[4] (James[3]) Pendleton *m.* —— Bowie *dau.* of Gov. Bowie of Maryland; issue:

i. John[5] *m.* —— Taylor; issue, James[6], John T.[6], Thomas[6], Catherine[6].

ii. Margaret[5] *m.* 1st R. Slaughter, 2d —— Morris.

iii. Nancy[5] *m.* 1st —— Brown, 2d Valentine Johnson; issue, James Bowie[6], Thomas M.[6] *m.* Jane Farmer. Their descendants in Illinois and Missouri.

iv. Catherine[5] *m.* Archibald Tutt.

v. James Bowie[5] *d.* unmarried.

vi. Thomas[5] *m.* —— Farmer.

vii. William[5] *m.* Nancy, *dau.* of Capt. John Strother.

viii. Catlett[5] *d.* unmarried.

ix. Elizabeth[5] *m.* Henry Pendleton, her cousin, and removed to Kentucky.

Issue of William[5] and Nancy (Strother) Pendleton:

i. John Strother[6] (Mem. of House of Del., Va., M. C., served seven years in diplomatic service) *m.* Lucy Ann Williams.

ii. Albert Gallatin[6] (House of Del., *d.* 1875) *m.* Elvira Chapman; issue, three daughters who married respectively P. W. Strother, Wm. Taliaferro and Crockett.

iii. James French[6] (Supt. Va. Penitentiary) *m.* Narcissa P. Cecil; issue, Albert G.[7], John S.[7], James F.[7], William C.[7], Edmund[7].

iv. William[6] *d.* young and unmarried.

v. French[6] *d.* young and unmarried.

Henry[4] (James[3]) Pendleton (Member of Culpeper Committee of Safety, 1775, and of Patriot Convention, 1775-6) *m.* —— Thomas of Orange Co.; issue:

i. Dau.[5] *m.* —— Browning; issue, dau. *m.* Capt. French Strother, now residing in Missouri.

ii. Dau.[5] *m.* —— Smith.

iii. Dau.[5] *m.* —— Green.

iv. Edward[5] *m.* Sarah Strother.

v. Henry[5] *m.* Elizabeth Pendleton, his cousin.

vi. Edmund[5] *m.* Elizabeth Ward; issue:

i. Edward[6] *d.* without issue.

ii. William[6] *d.* without issue.

iii. Daniel[6] *d.* without issue.

iv. Theodrick[6] settled in Clarke Co., Va.

v. Robert W.[6] resides in Baltimore, Md., (Pres. Valley R. R. Co.)

vi. Peter[6]. Peter is President of Valley R. R. Robert W. died a retired merchant in '58 or '59.

vii. George W.[6] removed to Arkansas, *d.*

viii. Mary Ann[6] *m.* Wm. Foushee who *d.*

ix. Elizabeth W.[6] *m.* E. B. Long of Baltimore who *d.*; issue, dau.[7] *m.* Geo. W. Williams.

Issue of John[2] and ——— (Tinsley) Pendleton.

i. Benjamin[3] emigrated immediately after the Revolutionary War to Kentucky.

ii. Isaac[3] emigrated immediately after the Revolutionary War to Kentucky.

iii. John[3] emigrated immediately after the Revolutionary War to Kentucky, where himself, wife and two children were captured by the Indians and never afterwards heard from.

iv. Edmund[3].

v. Richard[3] *m.* ——— Tinsley his first cousin; issue, William[4], Betty[4], Lucy[4], Sarah[4], James[4], Pauline[4], Reuben[4], Polly[4], Richard[4], Henry[4].

vi. Reuben[3] *m.* Ann Garland of Amherst Co., Va.

vii. James[3] *m.* ——— Rucker. Numerous descendants.

viii. William[3] *d.* unmarried.

ix. Polly[3] *m.* ——— Whitten.

x. Sarah[3] *m.* ——— Mahone.

xi. Frances[3] *m.* ——— Camden.

xii. Betty[3] *m.* ——— Baldock.

xiii. Margaret[3] *m.* ——— Miles.

Issue of Reuben[3] and Ann (Garland) Pendleton:

i. William Garland[4], Clerk of Richmond Chancery Court, Register of State Land Office 1814-23, member State Council, Proctor Univ. of Va., *m.* Mary G. Alexander of Campbell Co.

ii. James S.[4] *m.* ——— Aldridge, of Amherst Co., *d.* in California 1851.

iii. Nancy[4] *m.* Capt. ——— Ware.

iv. Sophia[4] *m.* ——— Powell.

v. Polly[4] *m.* 1st ——— Wills, 2d ——— Seay, 3d ——— Nowlin.

vi. Eliza[4] *m.* Walter Scott.

vii. Jane[4] *m.* —— Crow.

viii. Martha[4] *m.* 1st —— Lucas, 2d —— Stovall.

ix. Frances[4] *m.* —— Staples.

x. Harriet[4] *d.* unmarried.

xi. Micajah[4] (M. D.) *b.* 1796, *d.* Oct. 1861, M. D. U. of New York 1816, U. of Penn. 1819, *m.* 1822 Louisa Jane Davis *b.* Dec. 29, 1806, *d.* Sept. 21, 1840. (Great-granddaughter of Robert and —— (Hughes) Davis, who settled in Amherst about 1720 upon a tract of land numbering 10,000 acres. Their descendants by marriage are connected with the Beverleys, Byrds, Dudleys, Raglands, Burks, Ellises and other prominent Virginia families.) Micajah Pendleton *m.* 2d, 1844, Mary Ann Cooper.

Issue of William Garland[4] and Mary G. (Alexander) Pendleton :

i. Alexander[5], officer in the National Observatory, *d.*

ii. Stephen Taylor[5], Principal High School, Richmond.

iii. Douglas[5], engineer.

iv. Mary[5] *m.* —— Hightower.

v. Eliza *m.* —— Reid.

Issue of James Shepherd and —— (Aldridge) Pendleton :

i. Robert[5] (clerk of Amherst Co).

ii. James Shepherd[5] *m.* —— Mills, of Richmond, Va.

iii. Nancy[5] *m.* William H. Rose.

Issue of Micajah[4] and Louisa Jane (Davis) Pendleton, M. D., (his first marriage) :

i. Edmund[5] *m.* Cornelia Morgan, of Cinn., O. (now living at Buchanan in Botetourt Co., Va.) Issue: William W.[6], Lizzie C.[6], and E. Morgan[6].

ii. Ann Garland[5] *m.* Lewis Bough, of Amherst Co., who *d.* leaving issue, Cornelia P.[6] *m.* —— Clark, of Ga., Louisa Jane[6], Virginia Grove[6], Alice Dudley[6], Nannie Lewis[6].

iii. James Dudley (M. D.)[5] Assistant Clerk Virginia Senate, *m.* Feb. 22, 1853, Clara Pulliam *dau.* of William Rock, then living in Buchanan Co. Issue: William Dudley[6], R. Edmond D.[6]

Issue of Micajah[4] and Mary Ann (Cooper) Pendleton, M. D., his second marriage:

iv. William[5].

v. Charles[5] *d.* aged 7 years.

vi. Elizabeth[5].

vii. Walter[5].

viii. Louisa[5].

Issue of Thomas[5] (James[4]) and —— (Farmer) Pendleton:

i. William[6].

ii. James[6] *m.* —— Conner.

iii. Daniel[6] *m.* Simms.

iv. John[6].

v. Alexander[6].

vi. George W[6].

vii. Anne[6] *m.* John Menefee.

viii. Eliza[6] *m.* —— Haynoo.

Issue of Nathaniel[3] (Henry[2], Philip[1]) and —— (Clayton) Pendleton:

i. Nathaniel[4] *b.* 1746, *d.* in New York, Oct. 20, 1821. Entered Revolutionary army in 1775, aide-de-camp to Gen. Greene; prominent lawyer and jurist in New York; second of Alexander Hamilton in his duel with Aaron Burr; *m.* Susan Bard.

ii. William[4] *b.* 1748, settled in Berkeley Co. Va., and was a faithful lay-reader of the Church of England, as was also his son William[5] who was the father of the late Rev. William H. Pendleton.[6]

iii. Henry[4] *b.* 1750, *d.* in S. C. Jan. 1789. Eminent as jurist and patriot; numerous descendants in S. C.; Pendleton District in that State named in honor of him.

iv. Philip[4] *b.* 1752, Martinsburg, Va.

v. Mary[4] *m.* John Williams. (See Williams genealogy.) No issue.

vi. Elizabeth[4] *m.* Benjamin Tutt.

vii. Susanna[4] *m.* —— Wilson.

Issue of Nathaniel[4] and Susan (Bard) Pendleton:
i. Edmund H.[5] Judge, M. C. Left no issue.

ii. Nathaniel Greene[5] *b.* Savannah, Ga., Aug. 1793, *d.* June 16, 1861. Aide to Gen. Gaines 1813-16; member Ohio Senate 1825-6; M. C. 1840-2; father of Hon. Geo. H. Pendleton[6].

iii. John Bard[5], left no issue.

iv. James M.[5] *m.* Margaret Jones; issue Capt. James M[6].

v. Anne F[5] *m.* Archibald Rogers.

Issue of Philip[4] (Nathaniel[3]) and —— Pendleton:
i. Philip C.[5] (U. S. District Judge) *m.* ——; left issue, Philip[6], Edmund[6] (Judge Circuit Court), E. Boyd[6].

ii. Edmund[5], (Washington, D. C.) *m.* ——, issue Isaac Purnell[6], Serena[6] *m.* —— Dandridge.

iii. Anne[5] *m.* —— Kennedy.

iv. Sarah[5] *m.* 1st —— Hunter; issue, Hon. R. M. T. Hunter; *m.* 2d. —— Dandridge; issue, 7 children.

v. Maria[5] *m.* John R. Cooke (celebrated lawyer); issue, Phil. Pendleton (poet), John Esten (novelist).

vi. Elizabeth[5] *m.* —— Hunter.

Issue of Anne[5] (Pendleton) and —— Kennedy:

i. John Pendleton *b.* Baltimore, Oct. 25, 1795, *d.* Newport, R. I., Aug. 18, 1870. (LL.D. H. U. 1863, author and politician, M. C., Sec. U. S. Navy 1852, prolific writer.)

ii. Andrew[5].

iii. Philip P.[5]

iv. Anthony[5], U. S. Senator.

Issue of Elizabeth[5] (Pendleton) and —— Hunter:

i. Philip Pendleton[6].

ii. David[6].

iii. Andrew[6], Charlestown, W. Va. (distinguished lawyer.)

iv. Edmund P.[6]

v. Elizabeth[6] *m.* —— Strother; issue, Gen. David Hunter Strother, "Porte Crayon."

vi. Mary Matthews[6].

vii. Moses H.[6]

viii. Louisa Brooke[6].

ix. Nancy[6] *m.* Rev. John Hoge, D.D.; issue, John Blair (Circuit Judge W. Va.)

Issue of Elizabeth[4] (Pendleton, Nathaniel[3]) and Benjamin Tutt:

i. Mildred[5] *m.* Burkett Jett of Loudon Co., Va.

ii. Dau.[5] *m.* John Shackleford (for many years Commonwealth's Attorney, Culpeper Co., Va.)

iii. Dau.⁵ *m.* Capt. John Williams. (See Williams genealogy.)

iv. Dau.⁵ *m.* William Broaddus (Clerk of Culpeper Co., Va.)

v. Elizabeth⁵ *d.* unmarried.

vi. Anne⁵ *m.* Robert Catlett of Fauquier Co., Va., of which issue one dau. *m.* Lewis B. Williams, another Philip Williams (see Williams genealogy). Nathaniel P. *m.* Betty Breckinridge, Richard H. *m.* 1st Molly Patton, 2d Miss Gay, John R. *m.* 1st Miss Swann, 2d Miss Henry, and left two sons by last wife.

vii. Charles P.⁵ *m.* ——; issue, dau.⁶ *m.* Charles Bonnycastle (Prof. Univ. of Va.), another dau. *m.* Josiah Colston, another *m.* Major —— Throgmorton of Loudon Co.

Issue of ——⁵ (Tutt) and John Shackleford:
i. Henry⁶ (State Judge).
ii. B. Howard⁶ *d.*
iii. John L.⁶
iv. Dau.⁶ *m.* —— Gibson.
v. Dau.⁶ *m.* —— Spotswood.

Issue of Philip² (Philip¹) and Elizabeth (Pollard) Pendleton:
i. Benjamin³ *m.* Mary Macon.
ii. Dau.³

Issue of Benjamin³ and Mary (Macon) Pendleton:
i. James⁴ (Officer in the Rev. Army.)
ii. Philip⁴ from whom the Pendletons of King and Queen Co. are descended.
iii. Dau.⁴ *m.* —— Holmes.

Explanation of Arrangement and Abbreviations.

This genealogy is recorded in regular succession as to generation, and in the order of birth of the issue of each marriage, as nearly so, or as accurately as the information gathered has afforded; but as to the last there are doubtless errors. The number of generation is denoted by a small Arabic numeral placed on the right of each Christian name, and a little above the text, commencing with Philip Pendleton the emigrant and common ancestor of the family as Philip[1], the order of birth of his children being indicated by the Roman numerals i., ii., &c. To avoid confusion and to facilitate reference the descent is arranged lineally in the order presented by the second generation or issue of Philip[1], from whom for extended deduction we first take Henry[2], the data for such purpose not being within our knowledge as to his sisters preceding him. Abbreviations have been used as follows: *b.* born, *d.* died, *dau.* daughter, *m.* married. Such other forms, &c., as are used are so palpably self-indicative that they cannot fail to be intelligible to all.

THE SLAUGHTER FAMILY.

It is not worth while to trace this family to the stock from which they spring in England. We limit our notice to the two brothers who were first transplanted in this parish early in the eighteenth century. Robert and Francis Slaughter were the first church-wardens of St. Mark's Parish, chosen by the first vestry in 1731.

Robert's sons were: 1. Robert, 2. William, 3. Thomas, 4. Francis, 5. James, 6. Lawrence, 7. George.

o

The sons of Robert (the 2d) were: James, Charles, Gabriel, Jesse, and Augustine. William, son of 1st Robert m. Miss Zimmerman and moved to Jefferson County; children, Thomas, William, John, Gabriel, and Smith. William m. Miss Briscoe, and Smith m. Miss Crane of Jefferson, and represented that county for many years. Francis, son of Robert 1st, m. Miss Suggett, and represented Dunmore County (Shenandoah) before the Revolution.

Thomas, son of Robert 1st, m. Miss Robertson; children, Robert of the Grange m. Miss Stanton; children, Thomas, Henry, Stanton (High Sheriff) m. Miss Pickett; ch. Arthur, Augustine, William Stanton, and Martin of the Culpeper bar, who m. Miss Bolling of Petersburg. Anne, daughter of Stanton, m. Rittenhouse Stringfellow; children, Wm. Stanton, Martin, and Rev. Frank Stringfellow (Gen. Lee's famous scout), Augustine was surgeon in the Revolution. Sarah, daughter of Robert of the Grange, m. George Hamilton of Spotsylvania; children, Dr. Hugh Hamilton m. Miss Scott, Sarah (Mrs. Roots Thompson), Charlotte (Mrs. Dr. Thornton), Robert, who m. a daughter of Judge Brooke, Maria (Mrs. Page), Mrs. George Thornton of Newport, Ky., and Mrs. John L. Marye.

James, son of Robert 1st, commanded a regiment at the battle of G. Bridge. He m. Susan, daughter of Major Philip Clayton; children, 1. Capt. Philip Slaughter (b. 1758, d. 1849) m. first a daughter of French Strother (see Strother genealogy); children, 1. Mrs. Isaac H. Williams (see Williams genealogy), 2. Susan (Mrs. Dr. Maconickie), father of Mrs. Strother of Tennessee, 3. Mrs. Frank Conway; children, Dr. Philip C., Dr. Albert Conway, Mrs.

Robert Shepherd, and Mrs. P. Clayton. 4. Eliza (Mrs. J. B. Dade); children, Captain Townshend, Philip, and Mrs. Edward Smith. 5. Sally *m.* Philip, son of Judge Slaughter of Kentucky; *ch.* Dr. D. F. Slaughter of Shelbyville, Ky. 6. Daniel French Slaughter (late Senator) *m.* first Letitia, daughter of Gen. Wm. Madison (see Madison genealogy); children, Gen. James E. Slaughter and Major P. Slaughter. D. F. Slaughter *m.* second a daughter of Wm. Winston (see Winston genealogy), Captain Philip Slaughter *m.* second a daughter of Col. Thomas Towles; children, 7. Dr. Thomas T. Slaughter *m.* first Jane, daughter of Reynolds Chapman; children, Capt. Chapman Slaughter, Col. P. P. Slaughter (badly wounded at Richmond), Dr. Alfred Slaughter (Surgeon C. S. A.), Thomas (killed at Richmond), Lieut. Mercer Slaughter, James, deceased, Richard (C. S. N.). Dr. Thomas T. Slaughter *m.* second Miss Bradford; children, Robert and Jane. 8. Mary S., daughter of Capt. Philip Slaughter, *m.* Robert A. Thompson (grandson of Rev. John Thompson), M. C. of Virginia and Judge in California; children, Captain Reginald Thompson, Sarah E. (Mrs. Dr. Hine), Mercer (Mrs. Gen. Ord, U. S. A.), Robert and Thomas, Editors of Sonoma Democrat, California, and Frank, State Printer. 9. Rev. Philip Slaughter, D. D., *m.* daughter of Dr. Thos. Semmes of Alexandria. 10. Anne Mercer *m.* first Edward Robertson; *ch.* Cornelia (Mrs. Dr. Long); *ch.* Mary Mercer, Anne Mercer *m.* second Philip, son of Col. John S. Slaughter; children, Dr. Philip Slaughter, Thomas F. Slaughter, Bessie, and Mercer (killed in battle).

Samuel (son of Col. James Slaughter) *m.* first Miss Banks; children, 1. Emily *m.* S. K. Bradford; *ch.* 1.

S. S. Bradford *m.* Miss Walden of Fauquier, 2. Louisa
m. General Wright, U. S. A., 3. Robert, 4. Rose *m.*
Professor Nairn, Columbia College, New York, 5.
Maria Champe *m.* Mr. Van Schaik. 2. Col. William
Albert B. Slaughter *m.* daughter of Judge Slaughter;
ch. Mary. 3. Col. Henry Slaughter *m.* daughter of
William Long; *ch.* Burgess. 4. Maria *m.* Professor
Bailey of West Point; *ch.* Loring, Whittaker, and
S. Slaughter. 5. Louisa *m.* General Merrill, U. S. A.;
ch. Wm. Emory, Sam. Slaughter, Mary, Loring. 6.
Dr. P. C. Slaughter *m.* Miss McDowell; *ch.* Ella,
John, Clayton, Wood, and Clarie. 7. Isabella *m.*
Col. Burbank, U. S. A.; *ch.* Sully, Fanny, and another
son. 8. Lavinia *m.* Mr. Jack of Louisville, Ky.; *ch.*
Matilda, Frances, Rebecca, and others. Samuel
Slaughter *m.* second Miss Virginia Stanard (see
Carter genealogy); *ch.* 1. Columbia *m.* William Green,
LL.D., of Richmond, 2. Virginia *m.* Dr. Daniel
S. Green, U. S. and C. S. N., 3. Sally Champe *m.* Rev.
William F. Lockwood of Maryland; *ch.* Dr. Lock-
wood and others, 4. Marcia *m.* Major J. B. Stanard
(see Carter genealogy).

Thomas Smith (son of Col. James Slaughter), State
Senator and Jackson Elector, Ky., *b.* 1778, *d.* 1838,
m. Miss Bibb, children, 1. John of St. Louis left 3
sons and 2 daughters; 2. Thomas J., merchant,
New York, *m.* Miss Henry (relative of P. Henry),
children, 4 sons and 3 daughters (names not known
to the writer); James (son of Col. James), Judge, of
Bardstown, Ky., *m.* Miss Gray, children Philip,
James Clayton (orator and poet), Dr. Samuel
Slaughter of Cheneyville, La., Dr. Harvey Slaughter
of Elizabethtown, Ky., (names of wife and children
not known to writer) and Gustavus. Robert, (son

of Col. James) *m.* Margaret, daughter of James Pendleton of Culpeper, *ch.* John Pendleton (died in Cul-
peper), Philip, George, Clayton, James *m.* Miss Ferguson of Culpeper, *ch.* James Burr of Louisville, who
m. 1st daughter of Judge Carpenter of Bardstown, *m.*
second daughter of Rev. Frank Thornton. George
Clayton, son of Col. James, married and died in
Culpeper. Ann, daughter of Col. James, *m.* Reuben
Fry (see Fry genealogy). Another daughter *m.* a
McLaughlin, another *m.* Judge Speed, and another,
Bell. Lawrence, son of 1st Robert, *m.* daughter of
Col. John Field, killed in battle of Point Pleasant;
children, John F., Lawrence, George and Robert.
John F. *m.* first Miss Alexander of Prince William,
ch. Jane, lately died, *m.* second a daughter of Robert
of the Grange, *ch.* a son in Alabama. George, son
of Robert the 1st, *m.* a daughter of Col. John Field.
He raised one of the first companies of "minute-men
of Culpeper," and after the Revolutionary War went
to Kentucky with George Rogers Clarke, commanded a fort at Falls of Ohio, and was one of the
founders and first trustees of the City of Louisville,
died in Columbus (1815), no issue. James, son of
Robert the second, *m.* Miss Hampton. His brother
Charles *m.* Miss Poindexter of Louisa, and settled in
Campbell County; *ch.* John, Robert, Mary and
Elizabeth. 1. John *m.* Miss Armistead; *ch.* Charles,
Sarah and Pauline. Charles *m.* Miss Coleman and
moved to Tennessee. 2. Dr. Robert Slaughter *m.* a
daughter of Rice Garland; *ch.* 1. Charles (lawyer of
Lynchburg and member of State Convention) *m.*
Kate Garland; *ch.* Lilian, Mary, Charles A. and
Kate; 2. Dr. Samuel Slaughter *m.* Miss Henderson;
3. John F. (lawyer) *m.* Miss Harker; *ch.* Charles,

John F., Robert, Samuel, Edith and Susan; 4.
Austina *m.* R. W. Broadnax, *ch.* Mary, Celeste.

Gabriel, son of Robert 2d, *m.* first Miss Slaughter,
m. second Miss Hoard of Caroline; *ch.* John.
Gabriel was the Governor Slaughter of Kentucky,
and the officer who was so highly commended by
General Jackson for his gallantry in the battle of
New Orleans. Jesse, son of Robert 2d, *m.* Miss
Slaughter, and Augustine *m.* Miss Fisher and lived
near Harrodsburg, Ky.

Francis Slaughter, brother of Robert, and a
churchwarden of 1731, owned a large body of land,
including the site of the old glebe. He served as
vestryman from 1731 to his death. His sons were
Francis, John, Cadwallader and Reuben. Francis
and John both married daughters of Robert Coleman,
on whose land Culpeper C. H. was founded. Francis
2d had several sons, of whom only one (Francis) is
known. He married Miss Holloway, and his son
Henry (M. D.) moved to the south. Reuben, son of
Francis 1st, with his sons Goodrich, Joseph, William
and Robert, moved to Bedford, where Joseph married and has descendants (Harrises). Cadwallader,
son of Francis 1st, moved with his sons, Russell and
Presley, to Kentucky. John, son of Francis 1st, *m.*
Milly Coleman, had six sons. Robert *m.* the sister
of Governor Slaughter of Kentucky, and had two
sons, Charles and Edmund, and several daughters.
Cadwallader, son of John, *m.* first Miss Yancey, *m.*
second Miss Hampton. He went to Kentucky in
1809, with his sons, Richard, John H., Robert,
Edmund and Cadwallader, and several daughters.
Francis and Thomas K., sons of John, went to Kentucky. John S., son of John, *m.* Susan, daughter of

Capt. William Brown, and raised thirteen children. 1. Col. John Slaughter of Culpeper *m.* daughter of Major Gabriel Long, and had four daughters, Mrs. C. C. Connor, Mrs. Gabriel Long, Mrs. George Slaughter, and Emily. 2. William *m.* Miss Ficklin, children, Franklin *m.* Miss Gill, Montgomery *m.* Miss E. Lane Slaughter, J. Warren *m.* Miss Sallie Braxton, Elizabeth *m.* R. Garnett, Sallie *m.* John F. Ficklin, Jennie *m.* Dr. Kerfoot, Matilda and Eliza are with their mother in Fredericksburg. 3. Samuel, son of John S., *m.* Miss Allen. 4. Philip, son of John S., *m.* first Eliza, daughter of William Lane, *m.* second Mrs. Fletcher, *m.* third Mrs. Robertson. 5. Reuben, son of John S., *m.* Emily, daughter of R. Long of Baltimore, children, Albert *m.* Miss Rogers, Frank *m.* Miss Motley, Ann T. *m.* Dr. Boulware, and Maria *m.* Rev. Mr. Buckner of Caroline. 6. T. Jefferson, son of John S., *m.* daughter of Capt. R. Moore, children, Reuben *m.* Miss Turner, Susan *m.* Col. Coons, Ann *m.* Lieut. Wingfield, killed at Spotsylvania C. H. (1864). 7. Albert G., son of John S., (Commander U. S. N.) *m.* Miss Randall of Baltimore, children, Josephine, Emily *m.* Mr. Stuart of Baltimore, Kate *m.* Mr. Drake of Staunton, and Lewis (of the house of Majors, Russell & Waddell at Hong Kong, China). 8. James M., son of John S., *m.* Miss Long, child, Mollie *m.* Rev. J. G. Minnigerode of St. Mark's Parish. 9. Mary, daughter of John S. *m.* John S. Long of Kentucky. 10. Elizabeth, daughter of John S., *m.* Mr. Downman, and, with eleven children, lived in Kentucky. 11. Lucy, daughter of John S., *m.* first Thomas Long, *m.* second Gabriel Long, children, John S., Gabriel, Nancy, Susan, Ellen, Lucy, and Thomas. 12. Nancy, daughter of

John S., *m.* Reese Jury, children, John S. *m.* Miss
Wolfe, Lewis C. *m.* Miss Holt, and lives in New
Orleans, Mary *m.* Edward R. Gaines, children, Dr.
John Gaines, surgeon C. S. A., *m.* Miss Smith of Md.,
Edwina *m.* John Long of Ky., Catharine *m.* J. M.
Lewis, Betty *m.* Rev. Mr. Huff; Susan, Margaret, Lucy
and Frances are single.   13. Susan, daughter of John
S., *m.* Roberts Menefee and went to Missouri.

William, brother of John S. *m.* Lucy Brown;
children, 1. William *m.* Fanny Brown, and their son
Alfred is Principal of Prairie Home Institute, Mo.,
and their son, Capt. Daniel Slaughter, C. S. A.,
m. Miss Berry, and lives in Madison; 2. Catherine,
daughter of William, *m.* William Armstrong; children, John, William, Ringgold, Lucien and Edward,
and a daughter, Mary Ann; 3. John, son of William,
m. Miss Harper and moved to Zanesville, Ohio,
Reuben went to Tennessee, Gabriel to Missouri,
George *m.* first Miss Adams, *m.* second Miss Slaughter,
Elizabeth (Mrs. Yates) Ellen, daughter of William,
m. Benjamin Ficklin; children, Slaughter W. *m.*
Caroline Wilkins of Baltimore, Benjamin F. had an
adventurous life, and died in Georgetown, D. C.
Lucy Ann (Mrs. Brockman), Elizabeth (Mrs. Dun-
kum), Ellen (Mrs. Dr. Brown), Susan (Mrs. Dr.
Hardesty), Lucy, daughter of William, *m.* W. W.
Covington; children, John, Warren and William,
D. C.   The last was captain C. S. A.   Nancy,
daughter of William, *m.* G. W. Thomas, and their
daughter *m.* Fenton Henderson of Leesburg and left
several children.

Of the Slaughter family of Culpeper there were
seven officers of the Revolution.   Col. James and
Col. John were members of the Committee of Safety

of Culpeper. Robert, Francis, Col. Robert, Col. James, Thomas, Robert, Jr., Lawrence, Cadwallader, Samuel, William B., and Philip, Jr., were vestrymen of St. Mark's Parish.

Dr. R. Coleman Slaughter of Evansville, Indiana, and Thomas C. Slaughter of Corydon are descendants of the 1st Francis. Some members of the family may be interested in knowing that its chief seats in England were Hertfordshire, Gloucester, and Worcester, and that the first of the name who took up lands in Virginia were John 1620, Richard 1652, '55, '79, '89, '95, 1710; George 1710, '19, '32. Robert first churchwarden St. Mark's 1732-35.

THE SPOTSWOOD FAMILY.

Alexander Spotswood, Governor of Virginia, and Ann Butler his wife, had four children.

1. John *m.* (1745) Mary *dau.* of Wm. Dandridge of the British Navy, *ch.* 1. Alexander, General in the army of the Revolution, who *m.* Elizabeth *dau.* of Gen. Wm. Augustine Washington and niece of Gen. George Washington; their *ch.* were 1. John, Captain in the American Revolution, wounded at Brandywine, 2. George W., 3. William, 4. Elizabeth (Mrs. Page), 5. Mary (Mrs. Brooke), 6. Ann (Mrs. Taliaferro), 7. Henrietta (Mrs. Taliaferro), 8. Martha. Capt. John *m.* Sally Rowzie, *ch.* Mary, John, Susan, Robert, Dandridge, Norborne, Berkeley, Lucy and Ann.

Ann Catherine, *dau.* of the Governor, *m.* Bernard Moore, of Chelsea, King William Co., *ch.* Augustine *m.* Sarah Rind and their only dau. *m.* Carter Braxton; Bernard Moore, Jr., *m.* Lucy Ann Lieper, of Phila-

delphia, their *ch.* were Andrew, Thomas, Elizabeth
and Lucy. Elizabeth, *dau.* of Bernard Moore, Sr.,
m. John Walker, of Belvoir, Albemarle Co., *ch.*
Mildred *m.* Francis Kinloch, M. C., of South Carolina,
and their *ch.* Eliza *m.* Judge Hugh Nelson, of Belvoir.
(The tradition is that when Congress was sitting at
Philadelphia, Francis Kinloch met Mildred Walker
on the street as she was returning from her hair-
dresser, and fell in love with her at first sight and
afterwards married her.)

Ann Butler Moore *dau.* of Bernard Moore, Sr., *m.*
Charles Carter, of Shirley, *ch.* 1. Robert *m.* Mary
Nelson, of York, 2. Ann Hill *m.* Gen. Henry Lee (his
second wife), *ch.* 1. Charles Carter, 2. Robert Edward
(the great Confederate general), 3. Captain Sidney,
U. S. and C. S. Navy, 4. Ann, 5. Mildred. Bernard
Moore Carter, son of Charles Carter of Shirley and
Ann Butler Moore, *m.* Lucy *dau.* of Governor Henry
Lee and Matilda (his first wife). Catharine Spots-
wood Carter *m.* Carter Berkley, *ch.* Elizabeth, Ed-
mund and Farley. Williams Carter *m.* Charlotte
Foushee. Lucy Carter *m.* Nat Burwell, of Roanoke.

Dorothea Spotswood *dau.* of the Governor, *m.*
Captain Nat West Dandridge of the British Navy,
ch. 1. John *m.* Miss Goode, 2. Robert *m.* Miss Allen,
3. William *m.* Miss Bolling, 4. Nat *m.* Miss Watson,
5. Mary married Woodson Payne, 6. another
daughter *m.* Archy Payne, 7. another *m.* Philip
Payne, 8. Anna *m.* John Spotswood Moore, 9. Dorothea *m.* Patrick Henry, the orator (see Henry genealogy).

For other branches of this family see Spotswood
genealogy by Charles Campbell, the historian, a descendant of Gov. Spotswood.

The Preliminaries of Marriage in ante-Revolutionary Times.

The following correspondence will show how courtships were conducted by our forefathers. The patriarchal authority was recognized, and young folks did not make love until the preliminaries were arranged by their fathers. We are indebted to Mr. K. Nelson, a lineal descendant of the parties, for the original letters; and as the old folks have been dead for more than a hundred years, we presume no one's delicacy will be offended by the exposition of these illustrations of a past age. In the foregoing Spotswood genealogy will be found the relations of the parties to the past and the present generations.

May 27th, 1764.

DEAR SIR:—My son, Mr. John Walker, having informed me of his intention to pay his addresses to your daughter Elizabeth, if he should be agreeable to yourself, lady and daughter, it may not be amiss to inform you what I think myself able to afford for their support, in case of an union. My affairs are in an uncertain state; but I will promise one thousand pounds, to be paid in the year 1765, and one thousand pounds to be paid in 1766; and the further sum of two thousand pounds I promise to give him, but the uncertainty of my present affairs prevents my fixing on a time of payment: —the above sums are all to be in money or lands and other effects at the option of my said son, John Walker.

I am, Sir, your humble servant,

JOHN WALKER.

COL. BERNARD MOORE, Esq.,
    in King William.

28th May, 1764.

DEAR SIR:—Your son, Mr. John Walker, applied to me for leave to make his addresses to my daughter Elizabeth. I gave him leave, and told him at the same time that my affairs were in such a state that it was not in my power to pay him all the money this year that I intended to give my daughter, provided he succeeded; but would give him five hundred pounds next Spring, and five hundred pounds more as soon after as I could raise or get the money; which sums, you may depend, I will most punctually pay to him.

I am, Sir, your obedient servant,

BERNARD MOORE.

THE REV. JAMES STEVENSON.

The official history of Mr. Stevenson is given in the body of this work. He *m.* Fanny Littlepage, a sister of Gen. Lewis Littlepage, whose brief and brilliant career is delineated in this volume. He had nine children, viz:—James, Edward, Nancy, Jane, Sarah, Carter, Lewis, Robert, and Andrew. 1. James (M. D.) died in New Orleans, 2. Sarah *m.* Rev. John Woodville of St. Mark's, 3. Edward was lost at sea, 4. Jane was lost in the burning of the theatre at Richmond (in 1811), 5. Nancy never married, 6. Robert *m.* Miss Towles and lived in Lewisburg, Va.; children, Robert, James, Charles, and Fanny Littlepage. 7. Andrew Stevenson (Speaker of Congress and Minister to England) *m.* first Miss White, daughter of a clergyman of South Carolina. The Hon. John White Stevenson, late Governor of Kentucky and Senator of the U. S., is their son. Governor Stevenson *m.* Miss Winston. Hon. Andrew Stevenson *m.* second Sarah, daughter of John Coles and Miss Tucker, and their only child, a daughter, died young. Hon. Andrew Stevenson *m.* third Mary Shaaf of Georgetown, D. C. Lewis Stevenson, brother of Andrew, *m.* Miss Herndon; issue, James, William, and Fanny, who *m.* Dr. Wellford. Carter

Stevenson *m.* Miss Jane Herndon; issue, Fanny Arnotte (Mrs. Thompson Tyler), Isabella *m.* Mr. Carter, Jr. (General C. S. A.), Byrd, and Sally.

THE STROTHER FAMILY.

Some think this family of Scotch origin, and that it had then the prefix of Mac. Others insist that it is Saxon. General Dick Taylor, son of the President, whose mother was a Strother, says, as we learn from Judge Strother of Giles, that he had visited the old burial-ground of the family in the Isle of Thanet, County of Kent, England, and seen the name in its various transitions from its original form Straathor to its present orthography. However this may be, it has long had its present form in England, for Chaucer has a facetious tale of two Strothers, the orthography being the same then as now. The earliest date to which we have traced the name in Virginia is 1734, when Anthony Strother patented a tract of land under the double-top mountain in what was then St. Mark's Parish, and is now Bromfield in Madison. The family abounded in the county of Stafford. John Madison, clerk of Augusta, father of Bishop Madison, John Lewis, who so long represented the same county, and Gabriel Jones, "the Valley Lawyer," all married Misses Strother of Stafford. Jeremiah, who may have been the father or brother of Anthony, died in what was then Orange County, (Culpeper not being yet formed) in 1741, leaving his property to his wife Eleanor, and appointing his sons, James and William, executors. The will was attested by Francis Slaughter, G. Lightfoot and Catlett. His

P

children were James, William, Francis, Lawrence, Christopher, Robert, and several daughters. Francis married Miss Dabney and died 1752. He was the ancestor of Gen. Gaines, John S. Pendleton, Gen. D. Strother (Porte Crayon), Gen. Duff Green, and Capt. French Strother of Rappahannock. William married Mrs. Pannill and was the grandfather of Gen. Z. Taylor.

James, the eldest son, married Margaret, daughter of Daniel French of King George, whose son Daniel died in 1771. He gave property by deed to James Strother's children, who were French, James, and Mary (Mrs. Gray). James died in 1761 and left property to his son French. French Strother, the vestryman of St. Mark's, married Lucy, daughter of Robert Coleman. He lived where Coleman Beckham now lives. He became a vestryman in 1772, and churchwarden in 1780. He made himself very popular by releasing a Baptist minister who had been imprisoned by a Justice of the Peace, by substituting his man Tom in his place and letting him out at night. That fact is stated on the authority of Capt. P. Slaughter, who married his daughter. He represented the county for nearly 30 years in the General Assembly; was a member in 1776, and of the Convention of 1788-9, and voted against the Constitution and for the famous Resolutions of 1798-99. He was solicited to oppose Mr. Madison for Congress (see Rives' Madison), but Monroe became the candidate and was badly beaten. Monroe had only 9 votes in Orange, Madison 216; Culpeper, Monroe 103, Madison 256. Col. Frank Taylor in his diary says, " Col. Pendleton of Culpeper came to my house from meeting of Sheriffs in Charlottes-

ville, and he says Madison has 336 majority in
the district." In the State papers published by Dr.
Palmer there is a correspondence between him and
Jefferson in 1776 which would seem to show that he
had some local command, perhaps City Lieutenant.
He died on his way from the Senate in Richmond,
at Fredericksburg, and was buried there. His
executors were Capt. P. Slaughter and his son
Daniel French. His children were Daniel French,
who went to Kentucky and *m.* Miss Thompson, a
descendant of Rev. Jno. Thompson of St. Mark's;
George French, who represented this district in
Congress 1817-20, and moved to Missouri where he
died. Hon. Geo. F. Strother *m.* Sally, daughter of
Gen. James Williams; his son, the late James
French Strother, who was a member of the Legislature (Speaker) and of Congress, *m.* Elizabeth,
daughter of Major John Roberts; children, French,
late Superintendent of the Penitentiary. Captain
John, member of Assembly many years, *m.* daughter
of Dr. Payne. James French, Judge of Rappahan-
nock County, *m.* Miss Botts. Philip W., Judge and
Representative of Giles County, *m.* daughter of
Albert Pendleton.

Jeremiah Strother, late of Culpeper, who *m.* Miss
Clayton, and is the grandfather of the Rev. J. P.
Hansbrough, is of the same family. So also, we
suppose, was William Strother of Madison, who *m.*
Miss Medley, and whose daughter Louisa married
Rev. H. Stringfellow, and is the father of Rev. Horace
Stringfellow, D. D., of Montgomery, Ala., (who has
also a son, Rev. James Stringfellow, in the ministry),
and 2. of Charles S. Stringfellow, a leading member
of the Petersburg bar, 3. of the wife of La Fayette
Watkins, also of the Petersburg bar, and of others.

THE TAYLOR FAMILY.

The root of this family in Virginia was James Taylor, who, coming from Carlisle in England, settled on the Chesapeake Bay, and died in 1698. His daughter Mary *m.* first Henry Pendleton (see Pendleton genealogy), *m.* second Edward Watkins. His son John *m.* Catharine Pendleton, and was the father of 1. Edmund *m.* Anne Lewis, 2. of John, who *m.* Miss Lyne, 3. of James, who *m.* Anne Pollard, 4. of Philip, who *m.* Mary Walker, 5. of William, who *m.* Miss Anderson, 6. of Joseph, who *m.* Frances Anderson, 7. of Mary, who *m.* Mr. Penn, 8. of Catharine, who *m.* Penn, 9. of Isabella, who *m.* Samuel, father of the late Gen. Samuel Hopkins of Henderson, Kentucky, 10. of Elizabeth, who *m.* first Mr. Lewis, *m.* second Mr. Bullock.

James, son of 1st James, *m.* Martha Thompson; issue, 1. Zachary *m.* Elizabeth Lee, and their son Zachary *m.* Alice Chew, 2. Richard *m.* Sarah Strother, and was the father of Gen. Zachary Taylor (President), whose daughter Sarah Knox *m.* Jefferson Davis (President C. S.). The present Gen. Dick Taylor is a son of the President. Another son of James 2d, George, *m.* Rachael Gibson and had many sons, seven of whom were Revolutionary officers. George was the ancestor of many Kentuckians, among whom Dr. Frank Taylor, Major Wm. Taylor, and Edward M. Taylor of Oldham County, Samuel Taylor of Clark County, and Dr. Gibson Taylor of Union. Another son of James 2d, Charles, *m.* Sarah Conway, and was the father of Harriet, who *m.* Catlett Conway; another daughter, Matilda, *m.* William Moore, and another, Evelina, *m.* George Mor-

ton. Erasmus, son of James 2d, *m.* Jane Moore, and
1. their daughter Milly *m.* William Morton, uncle of
Hon. Jere. and Dr. George Morton, 2. Frances *m.*
Garland Burnley, 3. Elizabeth *m.* Andrew Glassell
(see Glassell genealogy), 4. Lucy *m.* Rev. Alex. Bal-
main, 5. John *m.* Ann Gilbert, 6. Jane *m.* C. P.
Howard, 7. Robert *m.* Frances Pendleton; issue, 1.
Robert *m.* Mary Taylor, 2. Milly *m.* Hay Taliaferro,
father of Jaquelin, of Dr. Edmund and Mrs. B.
Stanard. 3. Lucinda *m.* James Shepherd, 4. Jaquelin
P. *m.* Martha Richardson, 5. Jane *m.* John Hart, 6.
Dr. Edmund *m.* Mildred Turner; issue, 1. Elizabeth
m. Rev. Joseph Earnest, late Rector of St. Thomas
Parish, 2. Robenette *m.* Dr. Thomas Reeveley, 3.
Edmonia, 4. Lucy Jane (deceased), 5. Erasmus *m.*
Miss Ashby.

Alexander, son of 1st Robert *m.* Mildred C. Lindsay,
and their daughter Sally *m.* Col. John M. Patton.

Frances, daughter of James 2d, *m.* Ambrose Madison
(see Madison genealogy), Martha *m.* Chew, Tabitha
m. Wild, Hannah *m.* Battaile, Milly *m.* a Thomas.

James, son of James and grandson of James 1st, *m.*
Alice Thornton, and their son James *m.* first Ann
Hubbard, *m.* second Sarah Taliaferro, *m.* third Eliza
Conway and had a numerous posterity, among whom
are Capt. Robert Taliaferro of Louisville, Ky., and
others.

Major Frank Taylor, from whose diary we have
quoted so lengthily in this volume *m.* Ann Craddock;
issue, James, Thornton, Robert, Elizabeth, Sutton,
and Francis Craddock.

FAMILY OF THE REV. JOHN THOMPSON.

This gentleman was born at Muckamore Abbey near Belfast in Ireland, and came to Maryland a Presbyterian minister. I am indebted to Mrs. Murray Forbes for documentary proof of this fact in the form of a letter from the Rev. Jacob Henderson (Commissary) to the Bishop of London, dated Maryland, July 30th, 1739, in which he says:—"The bearer, Mr. Jno. Thompson, has been a Preacher in the Presbyterian way at Newtown, on the Eastern Shore of this Province; but was, by the distractions of the ministers and people of that persuasion, put upon considering the terms of communion in the Church of England; and I do verily believe, upon full conviction, has embraced it. He appears to be a person of great candor and sincerity. He has been intimate with the leading clergymen for some years, and your Lordship will perceive what a character they give him in their testimonials. When I was in the North of Ireland, I had a very good character given him from many people of different persuasions. He is desirous of Holy Orders, and has a nomination from the Rev. Mr. Williamson to be his assistant, and I recommend him for Holy Orders as a person not only very deserving, but one that I sincerely believe will be an ornament to our Church."

The Rev. Mr. Thompson, as we have seen, became Minister of St. Mark's Parish (1740), and married (1742) the widow of Governor Spotswood, by whom he had two children.

1. Ann (*b.* at Germanna 1744, *d.* 1815) *m.* Francis Thornton of the Falls. Their only son, Francis Thornton, *m.* Sally. daughter of Col. Innes; children,

1. Sally Innes *m.* Murray Forbes of Falmouth; children, 1. Jno. M. Forbes (of the Fauquier bar) *m.* a daughter of Dr. Semmes. 2. Delia *m.* Alfred Thornton, 3. Frank *m.* Mercer, daughter of Jno. Chew, 4. Dr. Wm. Smith Forbes *m.* in Philadelphia, 5. Alfred *m.* Miss Bastable, 6. Kate *m.* daughter of G. Bastable, 7. David, 8. Mrs. Dr. Taylor, and 9. Mrs. Stevens Mason, deceased.

2. Betsy, daughter of F. Thornton and Ann Thompson *m.* Dunbar of Falmouth; *ch.* Anna. 3. Polly *m.* Dr. Vass of Madison County, 4. Fanny *m.* Dr. Horace Buckner of Culpeper, 5. Milly *m* Col. Abram Maury of Madison, 6. Dolly *m.* Samuel Washington of Culpeper.

William, son of Rev. Jno. Thompson *m.* Sarah, *dau.* of Charles Carter of Cleve by his 2d wife Miss Byrd; children, 1. Charles Carter Byrd Thompson, Captain U. S. N., who *m.* in England; no issue. 2. Gillies *m.* Mary Carter; children, Charles, and a daughter reared by Mrs. Judge Brooke. 3. William *m.* first Betsy Strother of Culpeper, *m.* second Caroline *dau.* of John, son of Rev. John; children, 1. Ann, 2. Wm. Fitzhugh Thompson, father of Mrs. Carrie Thompson Williams of Henderson, Ky., and of William, who *m.* Delia *dau.* of Frank Thompson; *ch.* Maria.

Rev. Jno. Thompson *m.* second a *dau.* of Philip Rootes; children, 1. Hon. Philip Rootes Thompson of Culpeper, M. C. (1801–1807), *m.* daughter of Burkett Davenport, vestryman of St. Mark's; *ch.* 1. Eliza *m.* Thornton Fry; children, General Burkett Fry, C. S. A., Dr. Frank Fry, and Cornelia *m.* Jno. Lyddall Bacon, President of State Bank and other institutions, Richmond, Va. 2. Eleanor *m* Wm.

Thornton, son of Col. Wm. Thornton of Montpelier; *ch.* Dr. Thornton *m.* Charlotte Hamilton, Mrs. Andrew Glassell, Jr., Mrs. Charles Gibbs, and Philip Rootes *m.* Sarah Hamilton. 3. Burkett Davenport *m.* Miss Bostwick, 4. Philip Rootes, Jr., *m.* 1. *dau.* of Col. Wm. Thornton, 2. *m.* Sarah *dau.* of George Hamilton.

Hon. P. R. Thompson *m.* second a *dau.* of Robert Slaughter of the Grange, Culpeper; *ch.* 1. Dr. John Thompson *m.* a *dau.* of Dr. Geo. Thornton, 2. Hon. Robert A. Thompson, M. C. of Va., and Judge in California *m.* first Mary Smith, *dau.* of Captain P. Slaughter of Culpeper; children, Sarah E. *m.* Dr. Huie. 2. Mercer *m.* Gen. Ord, U. S. A., 3. Captain Reginald H. Thompson, C. S. A., lawyer, Louisville, Ky., *m.* Miss Thompson, 4. Robert *m.* Miss West, 5. Thomas *m.* (name unknown), 6. Frank *m.* Miss West. Robert and Thomas are editors of Sonoma Democrat, Santa Rosa, California, and Frank, State Printer. 3. Francis, son of Philip R. Thompson, *m.* Caroline, *dau.* of Dr. George Thornton; *ch.* Mrs. Jno. James Williams. 4. Benjamin, who *m.* Elizabeth *dau.* of Gen. Andrew Lewis, 5. Wm. Henry, who *m.* Elizabeth Huie.

John, son of Rev. John, *m.* 1784, Elizabeth *dau.* of Dr. Howison of Culpeper, and moved to Kentucky, 1793, and was afterwards Judge in Louisiana; children, six sons and six daughters, of whom Mildred Ann of Louisville, Ky., is the only survivor.

Mildred *dau.* of Rev. Jno. Thompson *m.* Capt. George Gray (Revolutionary officer), and their son, Jno. Thompson Gray, born at Culpeper C. H. *m.* Miss Ormsby, niece of the gallant General Weeden, and among their surviving children is Henry Weeden Gray of Louisville, Ky., *m.* Miss Peers.

Rev. John Thompson's will was recorded in Culpeper 16th Nov., 1792. Witnesses, Benjamin Johnson and Thomas Walker ; executors, Fielding Lewis, Jos. Jones, Wm. and Frank Thornton. He devised to his son William 1550 acres of land in Culpeper and 19 negroes. To his son John, 2000 acres and 15 negroes. To Francis Thornton and Ann his wife, 800 acres and "a negro wench Queen." To his daughter Mildred, all the money due from estate of Governor Spotswood. To his son Philip Rootes, 1979 acres on Summer Duck below Mount Poney and 12 negroes. To his wife, his mansion, his furniture, his coach, 600 acres of land and 18 negroes. To his sister Ann Neilson, a home and support. To his sons William and John, each a lot in Fredericksburg.

Col. William and Col. John Thornton were brothers of Francis Thornton of Falls, who married Ann, daughter of Rev. John Thompson. They were all sons of Francis Thornton the elder, who married Frances Gregory. Col. Wm. Thornton, who married Miss Washington, was the father of Dr. Philip Thornton, Dr. George Thornton, John, Howard, and Stuart Thornton. Francis the elder had also a son George, who was the father of Reuben, who married a niece of General Washington, and lived at Greenwood, near Germanna, and was the father of Charles Augustine Thornton, now of Enfield, North Carolina.

THE WILLIAMS FAMILY OF CULPEPER.

This family, in every generation staunch adherents of the Episcopal Church, is descended from Pierre Williams, sergeant-at-law of London. Three of his grandsons emigrated to America, John, William and Otho. John settled in South Carolina, William in Virginia, and Otho in Maryland. From him was descended General Otho H. Williams of the Revolution. William had two sons, John and William, who owned large tracts of land near Culpeper C. H. John died childless. William married a daughter of Philip Clayton, and left children John, James, Philip, William, and Mary. Of these—

John *m.* Miss Hite, *ch.* Isaac H., John and Ellen. Of these Isaac H., eminent as a lawyer, *m.* Lucy *dau.* of Capt. Philip Slaughter; *ch.* 1. Ophelia *m.* Rev. Geo. A. Smith of Alexandria. 2. P. French *m.* John M. Patton, acknowledged as head of the bar in Virginia in his day, and served in Congress with conspicuous ability for eight years. 3. Eleanor *m.* Dr. Hite of Amherst County. 4. Eliza died in girlhood. 5 and 6. Lucy Ann and Isaac H., who never married, and 7. John James *m.* Miss Thompson and is a leading lawyer in California.

Mrs. Smith's children were, 1. Isaac, a distinguished engineer in Oregon and California, and Capt. of Engineers in the late war. 2. George Hugh, Col. in the Confederate service. 3. Henry, Capt. in the same. 4. Mrs. Dunbar Brooke. 5. Eliza (Mrs. Corse). 6. Eleanor, deceased, and 7. Belle.

Mrs. Patton's children were, 1. Robert W., who died recently. 2. John M. *m.* Miss Taylor. 3. Isaac W. *m.* Miss Merritt. 4. Geo. S. *m.* Miss Glassell. 5. W. Tazewell. 6. Hugh M. *m.* Miss Bull of Orange. 7. James F. *m.* Miss Caperton *dau.* of Senator Caperton. 8. William M. *m.* Miss Jordan of Rockbridge. 9. Eliza W. *m.* John Gilmer of

Pittsylvania County. Of this family, Geo. S., Col. of 22d Virginia infantry, was killed by a shell while commanding a brigade at the battle of Winchester in 1864. W. Tazewell, Col. of 7th Virginia infantry, killed while leading that regiment in the memorable charge of Pickett's division on the heights of Gettysburg in 1863. John M., Col. of the 21st Virginia infantry, commanded a brigade from the battle of Winchester in 1862 to the close of the Valley campaign under Stonewall Jackson. Isaac W., Col. of a Louisiana regiment, was made prisoner at the fall of Vicksburg, and afterwards commanded one of the forts in Mobile Bay to the end of the war. Hugh M., a Lieutenant, was wounded at 2d battle of Manassas, and James F., a Lieutenant, was wounded at Cold Harbor.

Mrs. Hite's children were Isaac, Edmund, Fontaine, Mary and Eliza.

John James' children are Frank, Henry, Thornton.

The second son of John, the son of William, was named John, or as he was familiarly known "Captain Jack." He *m.* Miss Tutt. His *ch.* were John, who *m.* Miss Mason, and Mary Stevens, who *m.* Henry Porter. John died leaving two *ch.*, James and Mary, now living in Giles County, and Mrs. Porter moved to Tennessee.

The daughter of John, the son of William, was named Ellen and *m.* Nimrod Long, a soldier of the Revolution and Captain in 1812; *ch.* 1. Mrs. Turner, mother of Judge R. H. Turner and S. Smith Turner. 2. Mrs. Lovell, mother of Judge John T. Lovell of Front Royal, and 3. John.

James, the second son of William, entered the Revolutionary army in 1775, served throughout the war and attained the rank of Captain. In the war of 1812 he was Major General, and commanded the Virginia militia. He *m.* first Miss Green, *ch.* William, James and Sarah Green.

1. William *m.* Anne Stubblefield, of Orange Co., *ch.* James *m.* Rosalie Fitzhugh, George S. emigrated to Kentucky, William *m.* Miss Pannill, Ellen *m.* Ennis Adams, Anne *m.* Dr. Alfred Taliaferro, and their dau. *m.* James Vass, Fanny *m.* Joseph Pannill, Sarah G. *m.* E. S. Taliaferro, Lucy A. *m.* Thomas Fitzhugh, and Charles B. died unmarried.

2. James died at an early age.

3. Sarah *m.* George F. Strother (see Strother genealogy). The *ch.* of James, the second son of William by his second wife, were Fanny, Charles Bruce, William B., Lucy Ann, Philip and Elizabeth.

1. Fanny *m.* Fayette Ball and died childless, 2. Charles Bruce *m.* Ann M. Hackley, 3. Lucy Ann *m.* John S. Pendleton of Culpeper (see Pendleton genealogy), 4. Philip *m.* Mildred Catlett, and 5. Elizabeth *m.* Dr. George Morton.

Charles B. had a large family of children, viz: Fanny, second wife of E. S. Taliaferro, Dr. James Edward, who *m.* Miss Harrison, Bessie, who *m.* Geo. Reid, Janet B., who *m.* William L. Hill, Harriet, who *m.* C. D. Hill, and Charles W., a lawyer and member House of Delegates *m.* a *dau.* of Isaac Davenport of Richmond.

William B. had no family.

Lucy Ann (Mrs. Pendleton) died childless.

The children of Philip were Robert, Lieutenant-Colonel and Brevet-Brigadier General United States Army, who *m.* Mrs. Adele C. Douglas, widow of Senator Stephen A. Douglas, George M. who *m.* Miss Long of Baltimore, and Betty Bruce.

The children of Elizabeth were William J. and George Philip, both of whom died unmarried; Lucy P. who *m.* John C. Green, son of Judge John W. Green, and for nearly twenty years Commonwealth's Attorney for Culpeper, Jeremiah, who *m.* Miss Turner, Charles B. who *m.* Miss Dickinson, Thomas D. who *m.* Miss Pannill, and James W. who *m.* Miss Harper. John Pendleton died.

Philip, the third son of William, was for fifty-five years the clerk of the courts of Shenandoah County. He *m.* Miss Croutson, *ch.* 1. James *m.* Miss Ott, 2. Philip *m.* 1. Miss Hite, *m.* 2. Miss Dunbar of Winchester; 3. Samuel C., who represented Shenandoah County in the Legislature and Conventions of 1860 and 1861, and succeeded his father as clerk; 4. Ann *m.* Mr. Jones, 5. Lucy *m.* Capt. A. P. Hill of Culpeper, 6. Sarah *m.* Col. Travis J. Twyman, and 7. Ellen *m.* Rev. Dr. Boyd of Winchester. Of these James left a daughter who *m.* Mr. Miller. Philip, eminent as a lawyer and one of the most prominent laymen in the Episcopal Church of Virginia, left two *ch.* by his first wife, Philip C., a prominent physician of Baltimore, and Anne, who married T. T. Fauntleroy, of Winchester, and by his last wife six, 1. Mary L. *m.* Rev. James B. Avirett, 2. Philippa died young, 3. John J., a lawyer of Winchester, 4. T. Clayton, M. D., 5. Sally, and 6. Lucy.

Samuel C. *m.* a Miss Ott, of Woodstock, and left a large family, 1. James H. a prominent lawyer of Winchester, 2. Samuel C., Jr., and 3. William, lawyer (both of Woodstock), 4. Lucy *m.* Judge John T. Lovell of Front Royal, and was killed by lightning while visiting in Missouri, 5. Betty *m.* Thomas Marshall killed in battle 1863, 6. another daughter who *m.* L. Wagner, druggist of Richmond.

Q

Mrs. Hill and Mrs. Twyman died childless; Mrs. Boyd left three sons, Holmes, lawyer, and Philip, merchant of Winchester, and Hunter, a lawyer in Maryland.

The fourth son of William, William Clayton, was for many years a leading lawyer of Richmond. He *m.* Miss Burwell, *ch.* John Green, Lewis B. and Lucy.

1. John Green *m.* Miss Cringan of Richmond, *ch.* William Clayton, D. D., of Georgia, John G., a lawyer in Richmond, died unmarried, Channing M., Episcopal Bishop of Japan, Robert F., a merchant in Richmond, Mary Ogilvie *m.* Hubert P. Lefebore, principal of a flourishing female school at Richmond, and Alice *m.* Carter Harrison, a major in the Confederate army, killed at first Manassas in 1861. His second son Lewis B., the veteran Commonwealth's Attorney for Orange County, *m.* 1. Mary Catlett, *m.* 2. Charlotte Blair, *m.* 3. the widow O'Bannon, formerly Miss Riley of Winchester. He had no *ch.* by his second or third wife; those by his first wife were William G., Judge of Orange Co., *m.* Miss Roberta Hansbrough, Lewis B., Jr., Col. of 1st Virginia Infantry, killed at Gettysburg while leading the charge, Mary Blair *m.* Mr. Leigh of King William Co., Mildred P. *m.* R. S. Booton of Madison Co., John G. *m.* Miss Willis of Orange, Ann *m.* Mr. Caldwell of King William, and Alice.

Lucy the daughter *m.* J. Adams Smith, for many years the honored cashier of the Farmers' Bank of Virginia, *ch.* Bathurst, now living in Tenn.

Lucy the oldest *dau.* of William *m.* John Green and left one son John W. who was one of the judges of the Court of Appeals, and one of the ablest judges who ever sat there (see Green genealogy). Mary the youngest *dau.* of William, *m.* John Stevens, son of Gen. Stevens of the Revolution, and died childless.

THE WINSTON–HENRY GENEALOGY.

RICHMOND, VIRGINIA, *September* 21st, 1876.

MRS. DANIEL SLAUGHTER.

Dear Madam:—I have been informed that your maiden name was Winston, and that you have a family-tree. As I am very anxious to learn accurately the Winston ancestry of my grandfather, Patrick Henry, I trust you will pardon me for asking a copy of the tree, or if it is a very large one, of that part which relates to his ancestry.

I am, very respectfully,

WM. WIRT HENRY.

CULPEPER, VIRGINIA, *October* 10th, 1876.

DEAR SIR:

My sister, Mrs. Daniel Slaughter, has requested me to acknowledge the receipt of your letter of the 21st ultimo, and to answer it. The account of the Winston family in our possession was written for the satisfaction of her own family by my grandmother, whose maiden name was Lucy Coles, a granddaughter of Isaac Winston the emigrant; and she married her cousin Isaac Winston, a grandson of the same emigrant. I will compile a genealogy of the family from my grandmother's record, and from information of a later date, derived from other sources. I have compared her record with the old wills, also in our possession, and I find it correct for two generations.

Isaac Winston, the most remote ancestor of that

name that I can trace back to, was born in Yorkshire, England, in 1620. A grandson of his pursued his fortunes in Wales, where he had a large family. Three of his sons emigrated to America, and settled near Richmond, Virginia, in 1704. Their names were William, Isaac, and James. It is the genealogy of the descendants of Isaac, the second of these brothers, that my grandmother has written.

Isaac Winston, the emigrant, married Mary Dabney, and died in Hanover County in 1760, leaving six children, William, Isaac, Anthony, Lucy, Mary Ann, and Sarah. I do not mention them in the order of their births; on the contrary, I think Sarah, the last mentioned, was the oldest.

1. William, son of Isaac Winston, the emigrant, ("He was said to have been endowed with that rare kind of magnetic eloquence which rendered his nephew, Patrick Henry, so famous."—Campbell's History of Virginia, p. 520. See also Wirt's Life of Henry), *m.* Sarah Dabney, issue, Elizabeth, Edmund (Judge Winston) and Mary Ann. 1. Elizabeth *m.* Peter Fontaine; issue, 1. John *m.* Martha Henry *dau.* of Patrick Henry, issue, Patrick Henry (other children not known). 2. Sarah Fontaine *m.* Charles Rose; issue, John, Peter, Sarah and Alexander. 3. William Fontaine *m.* Ann Morris. 4. Mary Fontaine *m.* first Bowles Armstead; issue, William, Elizabeth, Mary and Peter; *m.* second John Lewis, a nephew of General Washington; issue, Frances, Howel and Mary Ann. (The other children of Peter Fontaine and Elizabeth Winston were James, Edmund, Judith and Susanna, but their marriages are not given in the record. The Rev. William Spotswood Fontaine, now of Reidsville, N. C., and the Rev. Edward Fontaine,

now of New Orleans, belong to this branch, and are grandsons of John Fontaine and his wife Martha Henry.) 2. Edmund (Judge Winston) *m.* first his cousin Alice Winston ; issue, 1. George *m.* Dorothea Henry *dau.* of Patrick Henry; issue, James, a distinguished lawyer and politician of Mo., (died in 1852). 2. Sarah *m.* Dr. Geo. Cabell. 3. Alice *m.* Frederick Cabell. 4. Mary *m.* Mr. Jones of Buckingham. 5. Edmund *m.* Eliza Wyat. Judge Edmund Winston *m.* second the widow of Patrick Henry, no issue. His descendants are scattered in N. C., Mo., and Miss. Dr. William Winston, now of Toccapola, Miss., is his great-grandson. 3. Mary Ann Winston *m.* Dr. John Walker ; issue, Benjamin, John, Frances and Edmund.

2. Isaac, son of Isaac Winston the emigrant, *m.* Marianna *dau.* of Rev. Peter Fontaine, Rector of Westover Parish, (great-great-grandson of John de la Fontaine, martyred in France A. D. 1563, ancestor of all the Fontaines and Maurys in Virginia) ; issue, two sons. 1. Peter (see Valentine Supplement to this genealogy). 2. Isaac *m.* his cousin Lucy Coles ; issue, Mrs. Garland Anderson, who left one son Alfred, who emigrated to Kentucky, Walter, Mrs. Armstead and Mrs. Dr. Beckwith, all of whom moved to Alabama years ago ; Dr. Isaac Winston of Alexandria, who survived all his children and left no grandchildren, and last William A. Winston, who *m.* Mary Wallace ; issue, 1. Walter died unmarried. 2. Martha *m.* Dr. Payne ; issue, William Henry. 3. Mary *m.* Daniel F. Slaughter ; issue, Mary, Eliza, Caroline, John and Daniel. 4. James *m.* in Cal. 5. Wallace. 6. Isaac (your correspondent). 7. Caroline *m.* John S. Hamilton ; issue, Hugh and Mary. 8. Arthur, and 9. Lucien.

3. Anthony, son of Isaac Winston the emigrant, *m.* Alice *dau.* of Col. Edmond Taylor of Caroline; issue, 1. Sarah died single. 2. Anthony (whose children moved to Ala., their names were John J., Anthony, Governor of that State, Edmund and Isaac, and a daughter, Mrs. Peters). 3. Alice *m.* Judge Edmund Winston. 4. Mary.

4. Lucy, *dau.* of Isaac Winston the emigrant, *m.* first William Dabney; issue, William; *m.* second William Coles; issue, 1. Walter *m.* Miss Darricott; issue, Walter. 2. Lucy *m.* Isaac Winston (as before mentioned). 3. Mary *m.* John Payne of Philadelphia; issue, Walter, William Temple and Isaac (all died unmarried). 4. Dorothea or Dolly *m.* first John Todd; issue, John Payne and William Temple (both died unmarried); *m.* second James Madison (President of the U. S.), no issue. 5. Lucy *m.* first George Washington, nephew of Gen. Washington; issue, George, William and Walter; *m.* second Thomas Todd of Kentucky. 6. Anne *m.* Richard Cutts of Washington City; issue, Mary, Richard and James Madison Cutts, whose *dau.* Adele *m.* first Stephen A. Douglas, Senator in Congress from Illinois, *m.* second General Robert Williams, U. S. Army. 7. Mary *m.* John G. Jackson; issue, Mary, and 8. John Payne *m.* Clarissa Wilcox; issue, sons and daughters in Kentucky.

5. Mary Ann, *dau.* of Isaac Winston the emigrant, *m.* John Coles, brother of William Coles; issue Walter, Isaac, Sarah, Mary and John. 1. Walter *m.* Mildred Lightfoot; issue, Mildred *m.* Col. Carrington, Sarah *m.* Mr. Bruce, and Isaac died unmarried. 2. Isaac (if he married, not known). 3. Sarah *m.* but no issue. 4. Mary *m.* Mr. Tucker; issue, a *dau.*

who *m*. Judge Carrington. 5. John *m*. Miss Tucker; issue, 1. John *m*. Miss Skipwith. 2. Walter *m*. Miss Cocke. 3. Isaac *m*. Miss Stricker. 4. Tucker *m*. Miss Skipwith. 5. Edward *m*. Miss Roberts. 6. Mary *m*. Robert Carter. 7. Rebecca *m*. Mr. Single-ton. 8. Sarah *m*. Andrew Stevenson (Minister to England). 9. Elizabeth never married. 10. Emily *m*. Mr. Rutherford.

6. Sarah, *dau.* of Isaac Winston the emigrant, *m*. first John Syme; issue, John; *m*. second John Henry, a Scotch gentleman; issue, 1. Jane *m*. Samuel Mere dith. 2. William *m*. but no issue. 3. Sarah (marriage not mentioned). 4. Patrick (Governor Henry) *m*. first Sarah Shelton, *m*. second Dorothea Dandridge. 5. Lucy *m*. Valentine Wood. 6. Mary *m*. Luke Bowyer. 7. Anne *m*. John Christian. 8. Elizabeth *m*. first Gen. Campbell, *m*. second Gen. Russell. 9. Susanna *m*. Thomas Madison.

I find from this genealogy that we are relations. My great-grandfather, Isaac Winston, and your great-grandmother, Sarah Winston, were brother and sister. I annex to the genealogy a copy of the will of our common ancestor, Isaac Winston the emigrant.

Very truly yours,

ISAAC WINSTON.

WM. WIRT HENRY, Esq ,
    Richmond, Va.

Supplement to the foregoing genealogy by Wm. Wirt Henry of Richmond:

Sarah, daughter of Isaac Winston the emigrant, *m*. first John Syme; issue, John, member of the House of Burgesses and of the Convention of 1775, one of his daughters *m*. a Fleming; and John Syme, once an editor in Virginia, was his descendant.

Sarah Syme *m.* second John Henry (a Scotchman, a nephew of Dr. William Robertson, the historian, and a cousin of Lord Brougham); issue:

1. Jane Henry *m.* Col. Samuel Meredith; issue, 1. Samuel *m.* Elizabeth *dau.* of Gen. John Breckenridge, 2. Sarah *m.* Col. Wm. Armstead, 3. Jane *m.* Hon. David S. Garland.

2. William Henry *m.* but died without issue.

3. Sarah Henry *m.* Thomas Thomas of Bristol, England.

4. Susanna Henry *m.* Gen. Thomas Madison. The Bowyers and Lewises of Botetourt County are descendants.

5. Mary Henry *m.* Mr. Bowyer.

6. Anne Henry *m.* Gen. Wm. Christian, killed by the Indians in Kentucky, one *dau. m.* Governor Pope of Kentucky. From Mrs. Christian are descended the Warfields, Bullitts, and Dickinsons of that State.

7. Elizabeth Henry *m.* Gen. William Campbell, the hero of King's Mountain; their only child Sarah *m.* Francis Preston; issue, 1. William C. Preston, the distinguished Senator in Congress from South Carolina, 2. Eliza Preston *m.* Gen. Carrington of Halifax Co., 3. Susan Preston *m.* Governor James McDowell, 4. Sophonisba Preston *m.* Rev. Robert J. Breckenridge, D. D., of Kentucky, 5. Sarah Preston *m.* Governor John B. Floyd, 6. Charles Campbell Preston, 7. Maria Preston *m.* John H. Preston, 8. Gen. John S. Preston (C. S. A.), 9. Col. Thomas L. Preston (C. S. A.), 10. Margaret Preston *m.* Gen. Wade Hampton of S. C. After the death of Gen. Campbell, his widow *m.* Gen. Wm. Russell.

8. Lucy Henry *m.* Valentine Wood of Goochland; issue, 1. Mary *m.* Major Stephen Southall of the

Revolutionary army ; issue, 1. Dr. Philip T. Southall, father of Professor Stephen O. Southall of the University of Virginia, 2. Valentine W. Southall, late of Charlottesville, father of William Southall, James C. Southall, V. W. Southall, Mrs. Charles Venable of the University of Va., and Mrs. Charles Sharpe of Norfolk. By a second marriage, the widow of Major Southall had issue, Joseph Stras and several daughters. 2. Martha, daughter of Valentine and Lucy Wood, *m.* Judge Peter Johnston of Prince Edward, a Lieutenant in the Army of the Revolution, and a distinguished Legislator and Judge; issue, 1. John Warfield Johnston, 2. Gen. Peter Carr Johnston, 3. Hon. Charles Clement Johnston, 4. Edward William Johnston, 5. Algernon Sidney Johnston, 6. Beverly Randolph Johnston, 7. Valentine Johnston, 8. Gen. Joseph Eggleston Johnston of the late Confederate army, 9. Benjamin Johnston, 10. Jane Wood Johnston who *m.* Henry Michel of Washington, D. C. (The daughters of Sarah Henry were women of remarkable talents.)

9. Patrick Henry *m.* first Sarah Shelton in 1754; issue, 1. Martha Henry *m.* John Fontaine; issue, Wm. Winston Fontaine, father of Rev. William Spotswood Fontaine, now of Reidsville, N. C. 2. Anne Henry *m.* Judge Spencer Roane of the Court of Appeals; issue, 1. Wm. H. Roane, U. S. Senator, who left one child, Mrs. Edward Harrison, 2. Fayette Roane, who moved to Kentucky and died, leaving a daughter. 3. Betsy Henry *m.* Philip Aylett of King William; issue, a daughter who *m.* Rev. Wm. Spotswood Fontaine, and a son Gen. Aylett, father of Patrick Henry Aylett, killed in the Capitol disaster, of Col. Wm. Aylett of King William, of Pattie

Aylett who *m.* Henry Ware of New York, and of
Rosalie Aylett who *m.* Mr. Sampson of Brooklyn. 4.
John Henry, who left one son, Edmund, who settled
in Tennessee. 5. William Henry died childless.
Patrick Henry *m.* second, 9th Oct. 1777, Dorothea
Dandridge, granddaughter of Governor Spotswood.
The issue by this marriage were 6. Dorothea Spots-
wood Henry *m.* George D. Winston; issue, Patrick,
George, Edward, Fayette, James, Edmund, Sally, and
Elvira. These went to North Carolina, Missouri and
Mississippi. 7. Sarah Butler Henry *m.* first Robert
Campbell, brother of Thomas Campbell the poet, no
issue; *m.* second Alex. Scott of Fauquier; issue, 1.
Henrietta *m.* Gen. Wm. H. Bailey of Louisiana, 2.
Catherine *m.* Dr. Robert Scott, 3. P. H. Scott *m.*
Mary Yancey and left six children. 8. Martha
Catherine Henry *m.* Edward Henry of Northumber-
land, son of Judge James Henry, and died leaving a
daughter, Dorothea Dandridge, who died unmarried.
9. Patrick Henry *m.* Elvira Cabell, daughter of Wm.
Cabell of Union Hill, Nelson County, and had issue
a daughter Elvira, who *m.* William H. Clark of
Halifax, and had issue, 1. Elvira C. *m.* Augustine
Claiborne, 2. Nannie *m.* Thomas Bruce, 3. John, 4.
Patrick, 5. Eliza *m.* Alfred Shields of Richmond, 6.
Martha *m.* Lyle Clark, 7. Ellen *m.* George Lee of
Richmond, 8. Rosa *m.* Mr. Wilkins.

10. Fayette Henry *m.* Miss Elcan, of Buckingham,
and died childless.

11. Alexander Spotswood Henry *m.* Paulina
Cabell *dau.* of Dr. George Cabell of Lynchburg.
Issue, 1. Geo. Fayette; 2. Patrick; 3. John Robert;
4. Lewis Cabell; 5. Sallie *m.* Dr. Geo. Cabell Car-
rington; 6. Paulina *m.* Mr. Jones; 7. Marion *m.*
Sam'l Tyree; 8. Maria Antoinette.

12. Nathaniel Henry *m.* Virginia Woodson. Issue, 1. Capt. P. M. Henry; 2. Lucy *m.* John Cardwell; 3. Mary *m.* Mr. Garrett; 4. Martha *m.* Mr. Ward; 5. Dorothea Virginia *m.* Mr. Beasely.

13. Richard Henry died in infancy.

14. Edward Winston Henry *m.* Jane Yuille. Issue, 1. Dr. Thomas Y. Henry; 2. Patrick Fayette; 3. Maria Rosalie *m.* Dr. William B. Lewis; 4. Lucy D. *m.* Mr. Leighton; 5. Celine *m.* Robert Catlett; 6. Ada B. *m.* John G. Smith; 7. Edward Winston.

15. John Henry *m.* Elvira McClelland, granddaughter of Col. Wm. Cabell of Union Hill. Issue, 1. Margaret Anne *m.* Wm. A. Miller; 2. Elvira M. *m.* first Jesse A. Higginbotham; *m.* second Alexander Taylor; 3. William Wirt Henry; 4. Dr. Thomas Stanhope Henry; 5. Laura *m.* Dr. James Carter; 6. Emma C. *m.* Major James B. Ferguson.

Supplement to the foregoing Winston genealogy by Edward V. Valentine, (the Virginia sculptor).

Peter Winston, son of Isaac Winston and Marianne Fontaine, *m.* Elizabeth Povall. Issue, 1. Isaac *m.* Miss Burton; 2. Mary Ann *m.* Alexander Jones; 3. Peter *m.* two sisters, Misses Jones; 4. Elizabeth *m.* Hesekiah Mosby; 5. Susanna *m.* Mr. Grubbs; 6. John Povall *m.* Miss Austin; 7. Sarah *m.* John Mosby; 8. William *m.* Martha Mosby; 9. Ann *m.* Benjamin Mosby.

The children of Alexander Jones and Mary Ann Winston were John Winston, Eliza and Gustavus.

John Winston Jones, (Speaker of the U. S. House of Representatives), *m.* Harriet Boisseau, issue, 1. Mary *m.* George W. Towns, (Governor of Georgia). Issue, Harriet Winston, Margaret, John, Mary Winston, Anna, Lou Morton and George W. 2. James B. Jones *m.* Ann Crawley Winston, daughter of Peter Winston, son of Peter, issue John Winston, Peter E., William Gustavus, Louisa Winston and Augustus Drewry; 3. Alexander Jones.

2. Eliza Jones *m.* John Mosby. Issue John A. Mosby.

3. Gustavus Jones *m.* Elizabeth, daughter of Wm. Winston of Half-Sink, Henrico County, and moved to Paducah, Ky.

The children of Benjamin Mosby and Ann Winston were 1. Peter Winston, 2. Elizabeth, 3. John O., 4. Robert P., 5. Mary Ann, 6. Sarah Winston, 7. Benjamin, 8. Lucy, 9. Patrick Henry, 10. William H., 11. Susanna Virginia.

Elizabeth Mosby *m.* Mann Valentine. Issue 1. Elizabeth Ann *m.* William F. Gray, 2. Mann S. *m.* Ann M. Gray, 3. Benjamin Batchelder, 4. William Winston, 5. Robert Mosby, 6. Mary Martha *m.* J. W. Woods, 7. Sarah Benetta, 8. Virginia Louisa, 9. Edward Virginius Valentine *m.* Alice C. Robinson.

P. B. Jones of Orange County belongs to this family, but the author does not know the connecting links.

REV. JOHN WOODVILLE, RECTOR OF ST. MARK'S.

He was born in the north of England, and was the son of a captain, either in the merchant service or Royal Navy. Rev. John Woodville *m.* Sarah, daughter of Rev. James Stevenson. Issue James Littlepage, born 1791, who *m.* Miss Mary Lewis and left one son, James Littlepage, who *m.* Miss Breckenridge of

Botetourt Co., Va. Fanny, daughter of Rev. John
Woodville, born 1793, *m.* William Payne, and their
son, Dr. John J. W. Payne of River Side, Tennessee,
m. first Martha V., daughter of William A. Winston
of Culpeper (see Winston genealogy), and *m.* second
Elizabeth R., daughter of Col. Rufus K. Anderson of
Alabama, a son of Col. William Anderson (U. S.
Infantry), Tennessee. William Payne, who *m.* Fanny
Woodville, and whose piety and devotion to the
Church is so touchingly described by Bishop Green
of Mississippi in his charge to the last Convention,
was a son of the old vestryman of St. Mark's, Richard
Payne of Culpeper, Va., who was the son of George
Payne of Westmoreland (1716), who was the son of
John Payne of Lancaster (1679), who was the son of
Richard Payne of Northumberland (1633), whose
father came to Virginia in 1620 (see Smith's History
of Virginia, p. 52). The Rev. J. Walker Woodville
(*b.* 1799) *m.* Miss Mary E. Carmach. Sarah Ann,
daughter of Rev. John Woodville, (*b.* 1802) died
single.

LIEUT.-GENERAL AMBROSE POWELL HILL.

Among the men of Culpeper who deserve commemoration is General Ambrose Powell Hill (one of
Jackson's favorite lieutenants), who illustrated his
knightly prowess on many a battle-field, sealing his
patriotism at last with the blood of martyrdom. He
was the son of the late Major Thomas Hill, and a
lineal descendant of Capt. Ambrose Powell, the old
vestryman of Bromfield Parish, Culpeper, in 1752.

R

THE BROADUS FAMILY.

Another man of mark to whom Culpeper gave birth, is the Rev. John A. Broadus, D. D., Professor in the Baptist College, Greenville, South Carolina, a scholar of rare culture, and a preacher who exemplifies many of the best precepts in his excellent work on the art of preaching with power. He is a son of Edmund Broadus, who so long represented Culpeper in the General Assembly. Edmund was the son of Thomas, who was the brother of the Revolutionary officers, Ensign James and Major William Broadus, vestryman and lay delegate, who married Mrs. Jones, the daughter of the first churchwarden of St. Mark's, Robert Slaughter. Their daughter Patsey married William Mills Thompson, vestryman of St. Mark's, who was the father of the Hon. Richard Wigginton Thompson, the present Secretary of the Navy. Major William Broadus married second Miss Richardson and left several children, among whom is Miss Sarah A. Broadus of Charlestown, W. Va. Major Broadus was Paymaster at Harper's Ferry when he died, about 1830.

The first Broadus of whom I find any trace in Culpeper was Edmund, who patented land in what is now Madison County in 1736. The Rev. William F. Broadus of Fredericksburg was a son of Thomas, and James M. Broadus of Alexandria is a son of Edmund, and brother of Dr. John A. Broadus. Wm. Broadus, clerk of Culpeper, was the son of Major Wm. Broadus.

Miscellaneous Items.

—•—

THE BROWN FAMILY.

There lies before me a patent for land in the South Fork of the Gourdvine River, from Lord Fairfax, proprietor of the Northern Neck, to John Brown; he paying every year the free rent of one shilling sterling for every 50 acres, on the Feast of St. Michael the Archangel. It is dated 22d June, in the 20th year of our Sovereign Lord George II., by the grace of God King of Great Britain, France and Ireland, and Defender of the Faith, A. D. 1749.

(Signed)   FAIRFAX.

This land was surveyed by Major Philip Clayton, and it adjoins the land of Thomas Howison and Wm. Brown. It appears in the vestry-book that Daniel Brown was sheriff and collector of the parish levy. Coleman Brown was clerk and lay reader in the church. Thomas Brown was undertaker of a chapel in the Little Fork; and Capt. Wm. Brown was the contractor for an addition to Buck Run Church. These are the ancestors of the late Armistead and Daniel Brown and their families.

MEDICAL MEN IN CULPEPER BEFORE THE REVOLUTION.

The vestries having charge of the poor, boarded them among the planters, and furnished them with

medical attention.   The first physician employed by
the vestries, as early as 1734, was Dr. Andrew Craig,
then Dr. Thomas Howison, then Dr. James Gibbs, and
in 1755 Dr. Michael Wallace, ancestor of the Winstons
now living in Culpeper, and of the Wallaces of
Fredericksburg and Stafford County.   Dr. Michael
Wallace was born in Scotland, and *apprenticed* in his
youth at Glasgow to Dr. Gustavus Brown of Port
Tobacco, Maryland, to learn medicine.   The inden-
ture is now in the possession of one of his descendants
in Kentucky.   That seems to have been the way
(before medical schools) to make a doctor.

THE LAWYERS.

Lawyers who served as counsel to the vestries of
St. Mark's were, 1st. Zachary Lewis **1731** to **1750**,
2d. John Mercer 1752, 3d. John Lewis 1754, and
lastly, Gabriel Jones, the eminent " Valley Lawyer,"
who married Miss Strother of Stafford County, sister
of Mrs. Madison, the mother of Bishop Madison.
The present Strother Jones of Frederick is the great-
grandson of Gabriel Jones the lawyer.   Mercer was
the author of Mercer's Abridgment of the Laws of
Virginia.   He was the father of Judge James
Mercer, of Ch. Fenton Mercer, and of John F.
Mercer, Governor of Maryland.

TOWNS IN CULPEPER.

The first town, by Act of Assembly, was Fairfax
in 1759.   The name has unhappily been changed to
Culpeper.   After the Revolution there was a furore
for towns, under the impression that they would
draw mechanics and increase trade.

STEVENSBURG

Was established in 1782, on 50 acres of land where William Bradley then lived. French Strother, B. Davenport, Robert Slaughter, Robert Pollard, and Richard Waugh were the first Trustees, all vestrymen but one. In 1799 the Academy was established by Act of Assembly, and its first Trustees were Robert Slaughter, Charles Carter, David Jameson, R. Zimmerman, Wm. Gray, Gabriel Gray, Philip Latham and Wm. C. Williams.

CLERKSBURG, NOT CLARKSBURG.

In 1798, 25 acres of James Baysy's land vested in Thomas Spilman, Henry Pendleton, Jr., Bywaters and Reid.

JEFFERSON.

On 25 acres of Joseph Coons' land, vested in John Fishback, Thomas Spilman, John Spilman, Thomas and Robert Freeman, P. Latham, F. Payne, F. F. Furgurson and John Dillard.

SPRINGFIELD.

On 25 acres of John Spilman's land, vested in John and Thomas Spilman, and Messrs. Matthews, Fletcher and Tapp. Clerksburg, Jefferson and Springfield are in the Little Fork. They yet survive, but have not realized the anticipations of their founders, whose names we have reproduced above.

JAMESTOWN.

It will be news to some that we have a Jamestown in Culpeper. 25 acres of land were set apart by the General Assembly to be called Jamestown, and

Gabriel Green, A. Haynie, and Messrs. Grant, Corbin and Howe were Trustees to lay it off into convenient lots and streets. Who will recognize in Jamestown our modest James City?

BRICK MAKING IN VIRGINIA.

The prevailing opinion that our colonial churches were built of imported brick is an error. As to those in the interior of the country, the transportation of the brick was an insuperable obstacle. It is possible that a few of the churches on tidewater may have been made of imported brick, but as to many of these there are unquestionable traces of brick-kilns very near them, in some cases within the churchyard. The following bill will show that bricks were made even at Williamsburg as early as 1708:

HENRY CARY *to the Council*, 1708.

150 loads of wood at 12s.—£6 7 6.
Moulding and burning 70,000 bricks at 3s. 6d. per M.
Laborer's work resetting and burning 3s. 3d.

VESTRYMEN OF ST. MARK'S.

The names of the old vestrymen will all be found in order in the text. The following is an imperfect enumeration of the successors:— The last vestry under the old regime (1785) was composed of the following persons, viz. French Strother, Sam. Clayton, Rd. Yancey, William Ball, James Pendleton, Burkett Davenport, Cadwallader Slaughter, Lawrence Slaughter, James Slaughter. Then followed P. R. Thompson, P. Slaughter, Jno. Jamieson, Rt. Slaughter, David Jamieson, G. Jones, Wigginton,

Wm. Broadus, Rd. Payne, Rt. Freeman, Thos. Free-
man, John Spilman, Thos. Spilman, Peter Hans-
brough, Isaac Winston, Waller Winston, Samuel
Slaughter, John Thom, Geo. Fitzhugh, Jno. Wharton,
W. Williams, Fayette Maury, Dr. Thos. Barbour,
Rt. A. Thompson, P. Slaughter, Jr., James Farish,
Moses Green, Spilman, Rd. Randolph, Wm. Payne,
S. R. Bradford, Garland Thompson, John Cooke
Green, Wm. B. Slaughter, Dr. A. Taliaferro, Rd.
Cunningham, T. S. Alcock, S. S. Bradford, Frank
Lightfoot, Jere. Morton, Geo. Morton, P. P. Nalle,
Jno. Knox, Downman, Dr. Hugh Hamilton, John
Porter, Rt. Stringfellow, Jas. W. Green, Jas. Williams,
L. P. Nelson, Thos. Freeman, Geo. Hamilton, Wallace
Nalle, Martin Stringfellow, S. Wallis, F. B. Nalle,
Rt. Davis, A. G. Taliaferro, C. C. Conway, P. B.
Jones, Jr., Rt. Maupin, J. P. Alexander, Jos. Wilmer,
Jr., Dr. Payne, Wm. S. Peyton, E. Keerl, Burrows,
J. W. Morton, Jas. Crawford, Spilman, Jas. Bowen,
Jr. These names are from memory and therefore
are not in exact order of time, and doubtless unin-
tentionally omit some who have been or are vestry-
men. The author has failed to receive the full list,
for which he asked repeatedly.

An analysis of the families of the old ministers
and vestrymen of St. Mark's yields some curious
results. Among their descendants were two Presidents of the United States, viz. Madison and Taylor;
a Justice of the Supreme Court of the United States,
viz. P. P. Barbour; several Governors of States, as
Barbour of Virginia, and Slaughter, Morehead and
Stevenson of Kentucky; several United States Sena-
tors, as Barbour of Virginia, Morehead and Stevenson

of Kentucky; members of Congress, P. K. Thompson,
Geo. F. Strother, Jno. S. Barbour, Jno. S. Pendleton,
Rt. A. Thompson, Jas. F. Strother, B. Johnson
Barbour, and Pendletons of Ohio; legislators and
judges of circuits in great numbers, among whom
Judges Pendleton of South Carolina, of New York
and Ohio, Judge Green of the Court of Appeals of
Virginia, and Judges Field, Shackleford, Williams,
&c. These are but a few of the examples of this
truth. It is also a curious fact that every Episcopal
minister within the bounds of the original St. Mark's
at this date, viz. Scott of Gordonsville, Hansbrough
of Orange, Slaughter, Minnegerode and Steptoe of
Culpeper, is a lineal descendant of the ante-revolu-
tionary vestrymen, or he married one of their lineal
descendants.

ERRATA.

P. 22, Note, next to last line, read *New Post* instead of Newport.

P. 97, read "The German people is a *potent*" instead of "political."

P. 106, Capt. Slaughter's Diary, read "I am this day 91 years old."

P. 137, 19th line from top, read "3. Andrew G. *m.* Georgie."

P. 141, 10th line from top, read *Hooe* instead of "Hove."

P. 175, 6th line from top, should read "5. Alfred *m.* daughter of G. Bastable, 6. Kate *m.* G. Bastable."

P. 177, 2d line from top, for "1792" read 1772.

P. 185, 17th line from top, read *Marianne*.

In map of route of Gov. Spotswood, "Mitchele Sta." should read *Mitchell's*.

The map on p. 27 is Mayo's map, by which the controversy between Lord Fairfax and the Crown was settled.

The plat facing p. 28 is General Washington's, when Surveyor of the County of Culpeper.